Scarlet Macaw

Scarlet Macaws as pets

Scarlet Macaws Keeping, Care, Pros and Cons
Housing, Diet and Health.

by

Roger Rodendale

# Table of Contents

# Introduction

The scarlet macaw is one of the largest of the macaw birds in the world. These birds are known for their gorgeous plumes that include bright colors like scarlet, yellow and deep blue. Scarlet macaws are wonderful companion birds as they simply love to be around people and get easily imprinted on human beings.

Believe it or not, these birds simply love to cuddle and be handled by people and are rather big suckers for attention. This is why, it is very important for people to understand the behavior and needs of these birds before they are brought into their homes.

The scarlet macaw is a highly intelligent bird. Research shows that they exhibit intelligence equivalent to that of a 4 year old child and have the emotional intelligence of a 2 year old toddler. Now, if that seems irrelevant to you, imagine having a 2 year old in your home all your life. You have to deal with possessiveness, tantrums and some moodiness along with the lovely things such as immense love and companionship. The key is to be able to treat the bird as you would treat a child.

If you are planning on bringing a scarlet macaw home, you have to remember that these birds are exotic which means that they have very specific requirements in terms of care, particularly nutrition. Before you bring the scarlet macaw or any such bird home, the most important thing that you need to do is read up all you can about the birds and the species. That way you can make them feel at home and make sure that their natural behavior is maintained throughout.

Birds like scarlet macaws require a lot of attention to keep their minds active. That is the secret to their well-being. Planning regular activities, keeping their mind diverted and making sure that they do not get bored is not as easy as it seems. So, you need to be a well-informed owner to know if you are really ready for a bird of this kind or not.

Every year rescue homes are filled with macaws that have been abandoned because the owners did not expect them to be so difficult to handle. These birds that are so heavily imprinted on humans that it takes them forever to recover. To make sure that you do not turn into one of these owners, you need to learn all you can about these birds.

This book is a comprehensive description of everything that you need to know about a scarlet macaw. It tells you about the best ways to choose a bird for your home, housing requirements, behavior, feeding, grooming and a lot more. The book also discusses in detail about the flipside of having a macaw so you can make a responsible decision.

If you think that you can handle the flaws that come with a scarlet macaw, you are sure to have a wonderful companion for the rest of your life!

# Chapter 1: Know the Breed

The Scarlet Macaw is the National Bird of Honduras. In Spanish this bird is called the La Guara Roja. It is one of the most popular birds in the Macaw family and makes for a wonderful pet thanks to its loving nature.

These birds are known by several names including Red-Yellow-Blue Macaws, Red and Yellow Macaws or Red breasted macaws.

The Scarlet Macaw is bred world over for its beautiful plumes. It is also among the largest of the Macaws making it a more prized possession to all owners. In fact, several zoos offer birds like the Scarlet Macaw as an attraction to tourists from across the globe. Today, there are also several attempts to conserve and restore the population of these birds primarily because they are victims of excessive trapping for pet trade.

## 1.Physical appearance

One thing that is most striking about the Scarlet Macaw is its sheer size. These birds are huge going up to 36 inches in length when measured from beak to the tip of the tail. The Scarlet Macaw is known for its graduated tail that also points towards the end.

These birds are also rather heavy, weighing up to 1 kg when fully grown. One distinctive characteristic of the male scarlet macaws is the size of their tail feathers. They are much longer in comparison to the tail feather of the females.

There is no mystery to the name of the bird. Most of the feathers are bright scarlet in color. The rump and the covert feathers of the tail are a contrasting light blue in color. The coverts of the upper wing comprise of bright yellow feathers. The end of the tail feathers, the upper side of the tail feather are dark blue in color. You will see a distinct dark read coloration with a tinge of gold shimmer on the flight feathers of the tail and the underside of the wings. Very rarely, you will notice that the birds have wings that are bright green in color.

The area around the eye up to the bill has distinct white skin that is bare and unfeathered. One the face patch you will see small areas of tiny white feathers. The mandibles of this bird are dual colored. While the lower one is a striking black color, the upper one has a pale horn shade. In case of the juveniles, the eyes are usually dark while adults have striking light yellow eyes. The colors of the bird make it extremely easy to spot in the wild as well.

In many cases people mistake a scarlet macaw for a green winged macaw. The latter is larger and is also known for the rather obvious red lines in the facial area. These birds also show no traces of yellow in their plumes.

The legs of the birds are a contrasting black color. The colors of a Scarlet macaw are bright and quite striking. A bird with these characteristics is considered to be in the best of health. The color bands can vary of course and the yellow may sometimes be found on the mind wing feathers while blue is seen on the tips.

Male and Female Macaws are not too different in their appearance. There are a few differences such as larger bills in case of the makes as well as longer feathers in case of the males.

## 2.Habitat and Range
The Scarlet Macaw is found almost on the entire stretch of the Amazon basin. The range extends from Peru in the east of the Andes all the way to Bolivia.

They also inhabit a large portion of Central America. These birds are seen from the extreme east of Mexico and the south of Mexico up to Panama and even areas of Belize and Guatemala. These birds are also seen in small populations on the Coiba island. They are also frequently spotted on the mainland of Panama. There are also two regions in Costa Rica namely the Peninsula de Osa and the Carara national Park.

The habitat of these birds is restricted mainly to the rainforest in the Amazonian belt. These birds are usually found on tall trees, particularly the deciduous trees. Most trees near the rivers in the areas mentioned above are inhabited by flocks of Scarlet Macaws. In addition to tree tops, you will also find Scarlet Macaws in subtropical rainforests, woodlands, savannahs and a few open areas in the Amazon belt. All in all, these birds like to live in areas that are moist and humid.

In the wild, it has been observed that these birds exhibit seasonal movements as per the availability of food.

The Scarlet Macaw has also been introduced to several urban areas in Europe, the United States as well as Latin America.

# 3.Taxonomy

The Scarlet Macaw belongs to a genus called Ara. This is one of the six genera of macaws that you are likely to find in South America and Central America. The scientific name of the bird is *Ara macao*. In the year 1758, Scarlet Macaws were first identified and described by Carl Linnaeus. The protonym of this species was *Psittacus macao*.

There are two subspecies of Scarlet Macaws that you can distinguish based on the color and the details on the feathers in the wings. They are:

- A.*macao macao:* This is the South American species. These birds are easily identified by the green tips on the secondary coverts. These birds are more common in Costa Rica, Central Nicaragua, southern and eastern parts of Colombia, Panama, Venezuela, Guiana, Brazil, eastern Peru, eastern Equador and northeastern Bolivia.
- A.*macao cuanoptera:* This sub-species was identified in the year 1995. Basically these are the North Central American Scarlet Macaws. In comparison to the other subspecies, these birds are larger and have a distinct blue color on the wings instead of green. These birds are seen in the stretch from South Mexico, all the way to Nicaragua. They are also commonly found in North Central America.

# 4. Behavior

Scarlet Macaws tend to get quite physical during play. They love to cuddle and be caressed. Positive interaction is very important for these birds to thrive in captivity. These birds will get very nippy and irritable if they are not mentally stimulated enough. You need to make sure that the bird has a lot of toys to chew on, particularly hard ones made of wood.

The observation of most owners of Scarlet Macaws is that these birds are rather misinterpreted. They are known to be aggressive and quite painful to manage. Yes, it is true that they are the hardest of all macaws to manage. But for those with some knowledge and experience with macaws, they are delightful birds to have at home.

Scarlet Macaws tend to be a lot more sensitive to the homes that they live in and the surroundings in general. They have a very short attention span and can just get diverted in a second from one thing to the next. As the owner, it is your job to make sure that your bird has a lot of stimulation and entertainment, failing which the bird can become poorly behaved.

In addition to that, socializing your macaw is really important. Training them well and encouraging positive behavior can be the best thing that you do for your Scarlet Macaw. Now, these birds are extremely inquisitive. So a nip on your finger is just their way of greeting. Sometimes this is mistaken for aggressive behavior while the bird is actually displaying affection. The only way you can help your bird be social and well behaved is by understanding what good behavior for a macaw means.

In fact, training can be highly beneficial for your bird. Research shows that Scarlet Macaws can even solve simple mathematics problems!

All in all, the Scarlet Macaw is a bird with great elegance. Even in the wild, these birds are known for being extremely dignified albeit a little noisy when they are in their flocks. They make the most wonderful pets and can be truly entertaining even to the owners.

## 5. History of Scarlet Macaws as pets

The colorful plumes and the engaging presence of these birds have made them popular pets for centuries. The history of macaws, in general, as pets go back to ancient civilizations. Back then, macaws were kept as pets as a token of status and prestige.

The Mexican macaws Comparative Osteology that was written by Lyndon L Hargrove shows us the relevance of the Scarlet Macaws and other species of macaws amongst the native tribes. This book, written in the 1970s mentions a few interesting detail about the history of the Scarlet Macaw as a pet.

These birds were extremely important for trade for the Indians who occupied areas around Arizona and New Mexico. The feathers of these gorgeous birds were traded in return for green stones around the 1500s. This was one of the earliest known positive influence of the Scarlet Macaw on a civilization.

Since the tribes benefitted from these birds, they also held them in very high regard. Later on during the 1700s, the interactions between native tribes and the Scarlet Macaws were further explored. Padre Verlarde, a priest from Spain was one of the earliest ones to record the domestication of these birds.

Scarlet Macaws were raised by the Pima Indians mostly for the feathers that were used in ornaments and also head-dresses. Documents are available for other tribes such as Pueblo Indians who also raised these birds for their feathers that were used extensively in native art.

As we discussed before, the Indians revered these birds because of their importance in their culture. Some even associated the Scarlet Macaws with high morality. In fact, anyone who was known to be poor in his character was forbidden from raising or even keeping a Scarlet Macaw in his home!

It is clear that the explorers of the New World fancied these birds for their beauty and took back specimens with them. Most of these birds were taken as presents to the royal families in Europe. Some of these birds were killed for sport and taken back as trophies or souvenirs from their explorations as well.

It was in the beginning of the 20th century that several macaws were imported to Europe and the United States. The domestication and captive breeding of these birds was affected severely by the first and Second World Wars. Then, there were several outbreaks of bird diseases that prevented people from having these birds as well.

It was only after WWII that these birds began to be imported as air transportation became a lot more accessible. That is when there was a surge in the domestication of scarlet macaws and other species of macaws.

There is very little information available about the breeding practices that followed after the macaws became more and more popular. But, one thing is for certain that these birds did not go unnoticed thanks to the vibrant plumes and remain among the most popular choice for pet birds even to this day.

## 6. What do Scarlet Macaws eat?

In the wild, Scarlet Macaws prefer to eat nuts and fruits. They will also supplement the diet with flowers and some nectar. One important factor about these birds' diet is that they will also consume fruits a lot before they are fully ripe. This is uncommon for other birds because they do not have beaks that are as strong as the Scarlet Macaws.

Fruits that are premature tend to have a skin that is tough. Therefore, the pulp is not easily accessible. Only a bird like the Scarlet Macaw that has a large beak can break through it.

In the wild this gives the Scarlet Macaws a competitive advantage as they tend to get access to certain foods even before other birds do.

These birds have a tough jaw that can break any tough nut open. Their bill also has a bigger range of movement, meaning that they get more power. This also increases the range of foods consumed by macaws as they get access to a larger variety of nuts. They have a rather unique structure inside the beak which lets them press any hard seed between the palate and the tongue to break it down. Then the seed is ground up to make it easy to digest.

Typically, the diet of the Scarlet Macaw is made up of pods, nuts, seeds, berries, figs and palm fruits. During the mating season, their need for protein increases tremendously making them consume larvae and insects as well.

One interesting thing to note about Scarlet Macaws is that they can consume seeds that are usually toxic for other birds. This is probably because these birds eat a large amount of clay that you can find on the banks of the rivers that they tend to inhabit. This neutralizes any moisture that they may have consumed. There are clay licks around these river beds that many tourists come to visit. In the Amazon basin itself, you will find almost 120 clay licks.

## 7. Vocalization
Scarlet Macaws have a very distinct harsh, deep and loud call. This can be carried a couple of kilometers when the bird really screams. Sometimes they can have a guttural squawk and harsh screeches. When they are aggressive, these birds even tend to growl slightly. Their vocalization is rather peculiar sometimes. They will make these sounds in quick intervals of three to four loud noises. After that they tend to remain completely silent.

You need to be prepared for loud screams in the morning or just at dusk. This is a natural behavior pattern for macaws that you need to be completely aware of before you decide to bring them home. If you feel like this could be a nuisance to you or your neighbors, you have to reconsider the option.

## 8. Conservation Status
Scarlet Macaws are listed as a threatened species by the CITES. They are among the 16 species of macaws that are listed in this category. Not only are these birds affected by human intervention in their natural environment but are also showing a decline in their reproductive abilities in the wild. Most clutches do not survive and birds may not mate because of the

unavailability of a proper nesting spot for the pairs. This makes it harder to conserve these birds and reintroduce them.

Some of the common causes for the decline of macaw population include:

**Pet Trade**
In places like Costa Rica, baby Scarlet Macaws are removed from their nests and are sold on the black market for prices ranging from $200 to a whopping $4000. In the United States alone, these birds are sold for $4000 per individual bird. This has made them very vulnerable to poaching. They are illegally traded to various parts of the world from their native habitat. One of the most affected periods was during the 1990s when the population of these birds dipped quite drastically!

**Habitat loss**
Another major cause for the population decline of these birds is rainforest destruction. These birds, as we discussed before, have very specific habitat requirements. A lot of poachers also cut down trees in order to gain access to the nests that are placed on the tall trees deep inside the rainforests. The biggest issue with deforestation is that these birds are unable to lay more eggs as they do not have nesting spots. Eventually, the number of young raised declines, leading to an irreversible drop in the number of Scarlet Macaws in their natural habitat.

There have been several conservation efforts to make sure that the number of these birds is restored in the wild. One of the most significant ones is the Ara Project that was started in Costa Rica in the year 1982.

This project began as a conservation center of these beautiful birds. Then, a lot of macaws that were confiscated from traders were brought in here. They were primarily donated by the Ministry of Environment and Energy. Birds were even given away by pet owners who could no longer care for them. Now, these birds were human imprinted and could not be released into the wild. So, they were rehabilitated and given the right conditions to reproduce. The young were then reintroduced slowly into the wild.

The decline of these birds is quite alarming. In Costa Rica, 85% of the area was occupied by these birds as reported by Forbes. However, there are only two isolated areas that these birds are seen in today. The largest population is seen in the Osa conservation area and the other one is the Central Pacific Conservation area. There are about 1200 individuals in the former while there are 450 in the latter. The alarming thing is not just the numbers but the fact that the breed pairs in the counter are a mere 35 and across the globe are just about 1000. Most of the conservation efforts related to collecting birds and rearing them in captivity. Releasing them into the wild after adequate training and rehabilitation has turned the species into an "active" one today in the wild.

The idea of releasing birds raised in captivity gained momentum in the year 1990. This mission was undertaken by several projects such as the Ara project and was supported by various collaborators.

The first series of releases were seen in the Northern part of Costa Rica. It began in the southern part of the country near the Curu Wildlife Refuge and in the Palo Verde region towards the north. Most of the birds were able to survive in the wild and were even able to breed actively. These birds were documented on a regular basis and it was found that they did quite well in the wild.

Subsequently, several releases were carried out across the globe. Community outreach was given a lot of priority to raise awareness. Then, the populations of these birds began to thrive and most even survived for several generations.

In the 1990s, the World Parrot Trust was established as an effort to protect all parrot and macaw species in the wild. The Scarlet Macaw was one of the species that was given a lot of importance during this time.

The conservation efforts of this organization include several educative programs for people, rehabilitation and consequent release of birds that were rescued, captive breeding followed by release etc. They have also worked with various partners to spread awareness about illegal trade of these birds to prevent people from unknowingly encouraging it.

There are several conservation efforts that are taking place world over by the continuous financial and logistical support that is available. Some areas that the WPT has put its focus onto include Costa Rica, Honduras, Belize and Mexico. In fact, the Ara project is also supported by the WPT to help rescue and care for the birds.

There are several projects that WPT is supporting world over to release parrots into the wild. Some of them include that of the Hondurian Institute of Anthropology and History, the Macaw Mountain Bird Park and Nature Reserve and the Copan Association. These efforts have been extremely successful in improving the numbers of these birds.

In the future, the WTP proposes to provide support to local groups that are involved in protecting the birds and preventing wildlife trade. They will also focus on areas where the birds have been declared locally extinct. Tracking nests of released birds is a big part of these conservation efforts. Funds are raised to make sure that the birds are kept in great condition while being rehabilitated.

Although the bird is not completely out of danger of extinction, the positive outcomes of these projects provide a lot of hope for the future. There is a steady improvement in the numbers of these birds in the wild.

## 9. Scarlet Macaw v/s Green Macaw

One bird that is very similar to the Scarlet macaw is the Green Macaw. These birds are often mistaken for the other. Although there are significant differences between the two species, the lack of knowledge causes the confusion.

If you want to bring a Scarlet Macaw home, you should be able to tell the difference. If not you may have a bird that you find difficult to manage because you do not understand the habits and behavior.

Here are the main differences between the two birds:

• **The upper wings:** In case of the Green Winged Macaw, the upper wing has green covert feathers. In case of the Scarlet Macaw this is either yellow or yellow and green.
• **Plumage:** The plumage of the Green Winged Macaw is much lighter than the Scarlet Macaw.
• **The tail**: In case of the Scarlet Macaw, it has a red tipped tail and the tail is also longer in case of the latter.
• **The face:** Green Winged Macaws have small red feathered stripes around the eye. The rest of the face is bare white skin. In case of the Scarlet Macaw, the face is filled with red feathers only one the head while the face has bare skin all over.

• **Size:** The Scarlet Macaw is noticeably stronger than the Green Winged Macaw. This is most noticeable when you see them side my side.

When you decide to bring home a Scarlet Macaw, you should be able to notice these differences. If not, you can even take an experienced scarlet owner with you to pick a bird for you.

# Chapter 2: Buying a Scarlet Macaw

There are several things that you need to consider when you decide to bring home a Scarlet Macaw. These birds are extremely popular because of their size and, of course, their personality. But, if these are the only reasons for your contemplating to invest in one of these beauties, it is better that you research a little more about the bird before you take a decision.

In this chapter, we will discuss in detail about the various options that you have to source these birds and the considerations before you invest in a bird like the Scarlet Macaw.

## 1. Finding a breeder

A Scarlet Macaw costs anything between $8000-10000 or £4000-5000. This lists them under the world's most expensive pets. So, when you are getting a bird home, you need to make sure that you have the right source so that you have a bird that is in good health.

Always choose a breeder who specializes in Scarlet Macaws. The issue with Scarlet Macaws is that they are not prolific breeders. It is quite common to have several unfertilized clutches or death of the chicks immediately after hatching. So, a breeder who specializes in these birds would have spent a lot of time researching about the species and ensuring that they are kept in the best health possible. They will also be well aware of the behavior of these birds. So, they can be your most important support system while raising your Scarlet Macaw. However, you need to make sure that the breeder you are dealing with is not someone who is exploiting the bird for commercial purposes and is certainly not involved in any form of illegal pet trading.

The most important sign of a good breeder is his or her interest in giving the birds a good life. These are the signs that you need to look for when you visit the breeder:

### How is the housing of the bird?

Not just Scarlet Macaws, any bird requires enough room to be able to spread his wings and fly around a little in his housing area. If you feel like the birds are in a space that is too crammed or too dingy, it shows a lack of interest on the part of the breeder.

Even if it is a mixed aviary with several macaws, the birds should have enough room to move around freely and just be relaxed. If you see that the birds do not have room to perch or are practically over one another, you need to move on to the next breeder. Not only is this a sign of negligence but is also a warning sign that the birds could be harboring several diseases.

Lastly, check the hygiene of the set up. Are the aviaries too smelly and dirty? Then there are chances that the birds have been exposed to bacteria and fungi that can cause deadly diseases to the bird. The food bowls and water containers should be clean with no traces of feathers or bird poop in them. In addition to that the floor and the bars of the cage should both be free from any dried feces. Any dampness in the cage is a threat to the bird's health and should be taken notice of.

**Do the birds look well fed?**

This is yet another reason why it is best to go to a breeder who deals especially in Scarlet Macaws. These birds have a special diet that is rich in fat. If you fail to provide them with this diet, they tend to have poor feather quality and will also be very skinny.

The size of the Scarlet Macaws makes it very easy to identify a bird that is undernourished. Now, watch the chest of the bird when it is breathing. If you are able to see the sternum and the rib cage very clearly, it is a sign of poor eating. Normally, the sternum is only seen as a faint line running down the center of the chest. If it is prominent, it means that the bird is not well fed.

**How is the color of the skin around the eyes?**

Normally, Scarlet Macaws will have a bright yellow patch of skin around the eyes. If the birds are kept outside, the color is brighter. When the birds have been kept inside, the color is a little pale. However, if the color of this skin is whitish, it is a sign of poor health.

**Are the birds too noisy?**

In case of Scarlet Macaws, just good housing and food isn't enough to keep them healthy. These birds are extremely intelligent and require a good amount of mental stimulation. They are also sensitive to negligence and lack of a partner that they can bond with.

16

Yes, like all parrots, they have a tendency to screech from time to time. However, a macaw who is persistent with the screaming is either bored or is simply seeking attention. Both can lead to severe behavior problems in the future.

The behavior is not as much of a problem as the fact that your breeder would allow the birds to feel neglected and unhappy. Then, the breeder is not really interested in what the birds really need.

## If you are getting a pair home, do they appear bonded?

There are several breeders who will just sell you two birds claiming that they are a bonded pair. Now, if you bring home birds that are not really bonded, there are chances that one of them will get aggressive and territorial and may even harm the other bird severely.

You must insist on DNA test reports that prove that one is male and the other is female as sexing these birds visually is impossible. Remember, two birds is double the investment. So it does not hurt to be entirely sure.

Once you find that your breeder seems to have a genuine interest in the birds, the next step is to take some measures to ensure that you are investing in the right place:

## Ask for a health certificate

All good breeders will provide a health certificate as proof that the bird was in good health when purchased. You will have to get your bird tested by a certified avian vet in order to get a health certificate validated. This health certificate allows you to return the bird to the breeder in case any disease is detected in this test. You also have a 90 day return policy that allows you to exchange the bird or get a full refund if there are any issues with the bird within 90 days of purchase.

Make sure that your bird is tested for Psittacosis. This is one of the leading causes of death in pet parrots. If your bird has this condition, it can spread it to other birds in your household too. If Psittacosis is detected, most breeders will give your entire money back to you.

## Check the history of your breeder's aviary

You can learn more about the aviary from the breeder and his staff. Try to understand if there were any outbreaks of diseases like Macaw Wasting Disease in the aviary in the past. Most breeders will deny it, of course. That is why you need to do your research by talking to vendors like the food and housing providers or even pet stores that the aviary may be providing specimens for.

In case you do find out about the outbreak from a third source, do not invest on this breeder. However, if the breeder owns up to the outbreak and is able to tell you how they controlled the disease within the aviary, he is certainly trustworthy.

There are several bird clubs who can testify for well-known breeders. You can even look for more information about your breeder's practices in these arenas and forums.

**Ask for references**

The best people to check up for more information about the breeder are the people who have bought pets from him. Any good breeder will be happy to visit one of his babies with you. If your breeder is hesitant to share this information, it is a sign that something is amiss.

References always work to your advantage in the future. These people will also become valuable contacts to have when you begin your journey with your own Scarlet Macaw.

Other signs of a trustworthy breeder are a fully functioning website, the ability of his team to work with the birds, his confidence in answering your queries and the general behavior of the individual around these birds. If you see that the breeder is caring and gentle, he may have taken good care of the birds.

Someone who has put in a lot of efforts in the bird will also need to be sure that he finds a good home. So, if your breeder asks you a few questions about your schedule and your plans on caring for the bird, it is a good thing. On the other hand, if he is only keen on making a sale, he is probably only commercially inclined.

A knowledgeable breeder along with a good avian vet are very important in your journey with a Scarlet Macaw. These birds have specific demands in terms of the diet and the ambience that they are kept in. A good breeder will help you with everything that you need as he is genuinely concerned about the well-being of his birds.

**a.Choose handfed birds**
If you are a first time buyer, insist on birds that have been handfed only. While it is possible to train Scarlet Macaws pretty easily considering their

intelligence, it is not really a good idea to train the birds after you have brought them into your home if you are a first time owner.

Now, our fingers and hands are pretty intimidating to birds. They also closely resemble branches of the trees or even the worms to most birds. They are likely to take a bite on them or just nibble on your fingers as an attempt to find a suitable perch. With smaller birds, this is acceptable. But if you bring home a juvenile or adult Scarlet Macaw, even the slightest friendly nibble can cause some serious damage.

These birds have a very strong biting ability and are known to easily crack the hardest nuts with great ease. Therefore, new owners should look for birds that have been handfed.

When they are younger, hand feeding these birds makes them used to the way out hands move. These birds are comfortable being handled and are less likely to perceive your fingers as a threat. It is also much easier to train these birds.

However, if you want to hand train the birds yourself, it is a good idea to bring home a baby. These birds are smaller and their bite will not hurt you as much. Of course, with younger birds, they are not as easily threatened. They tend to be more welcoming because of their curiosity towards new experiences.

For first time owners, handfed birds are the easier and safer options. If you adopt or want to bring home an adult bird who is not hand tamed, it is a good idea to look for a professional trainer who can help you train the bird.

### b. Buying from an online breeder
Many pet owners believe that buying from an online breeder is actually quite a good idea. It certainly is if the breeder is well known and has a reputation for selling only healthy birds. However, with a bird as expensive as the Scarlet Macaw, this is not a risk that is worth taking.

Now, you need to understand that with online breeders, you have no way of knowing how the birds have been maintained. There could be several pictures on their website. However, unless you can check the place yourself or can have a friend or family member do that for you, it is advisable not to invest in online purchases.

There is a 50% chance that you will get a beautiful, healthy bird. However the other 50% is a risk that you cannot take with Scarlet Macaws. Even if you pay half the price of the bird as an advance, it is a good amount of money.

With online breeders, even a reputable one is not advisable for birds like this. You see, after the bird has been shipped, there is not much control that the breeder has over the travelling conditions of the bird.

There are chances that you will get a fatigued bird whose health has been compromised due to lack of food or proper transport conditions.

If you insist on online purchase of a Scarlet Macaw for convenience purposes, here are a few things that you need to keep in mind:

- Only opt for breeders who can be recommended by friends and family. They should have personally made a purchase for the recommendation to be of value to you.
- Do not choose a breeder who is too far away from your city. It is best to choose someone in a city that you can reach in under 5 hours by flight. If your birds need to spend long hours on the flight, it is not good for his health.
- Ask for a health certificate with your bird. Tests should be based on blood and fecal samples. That helps you ensure that there are no chances of psittacosis in your Scarlet Macaw.
- Ask your breeders to provide you with contacts of people that he has shipped birds to in the past. Any good breeder will share this information easily.

Of course, with online purchases, scams cannot be neglected. There are several individuals who will try to make a quick buck out of your requirement. Now, when you are looking online, you are going to look in a search engine most probably. This notifies people who run fake websites.

There have been instances when potential owners have received pictures of birds that belong to someone else. In these pictures, you will even see the owner of the bird that these scam websites claim to themselves.

You can catch a scam pretty easily. They will approach you persistently to make a sale. In addition to that, they will ask you to pay small amounts in intervals. They will keep on adding new expenses like insurance, transport etc. An authorized breeder will know what all expenses are involved and will give you a full invoice and costing for transporting the bird.

When a breeder approaches you to make a sale, make sure you ask them questions about Scarlet Macaws. Ask them about the breeding season of the bird, the diet, the care required etc. These questions should be asked over the phone to make sure that they are not looking for answers online.

Anyone interested in just scamming you will have no idea about these birds most often.

Lastly, you need to ask them for contacts of people that they have already sold birds to. If they are reluctant or do not share this information for any other reason, you need to become aware that they are trying to scam you.

People have lost hundreds of dollars trying to make online purchases. Most of these websites will be pulled down within days of "making a sale" or getting an advance from people. Remember, never pay the full amount to a breeder until you receive the bird in good condition when you are placing an order online.

## 2. Adopting a Scarlet Macaw

If you are a slightly experienced bird owner, you are probably ready to adopt a Scarlet Macaw. What you need to know about adopting any bird is that you are probably going to find an adult bird that also has a history of abandonment or even abuse. These birds tend to be shy or aggressive depending upon the experiences that they have had in the past.

With adoption, you need to know that the birds need additional care which you will be able to provide only after you have some experience with the birds. You may also have to spend more money on the medical treatment of these birds in order to bring them back to good health. Since the Scarlet Macaw is also a rare species, there are several policies regarding the adoption of these birds.

Adoption agencies that work with species like the Scarlet Macaw are very particular about the care that the birds are going to receive. Therefore, they have two options for all the birds that come under their care. One is lifetime sanctuary where the birds are kept in the adoption center till they live. This is normally done when the bird requires that kind of attention because of some health issue that it has. In addition to that, when some people give their birds up, they request lifetime care to make sure that the bird is in good hands.

The second option is when the birds are put out for adoption. Now, with the Scarlet Macaw, they are exceptionally careful about the adoption process as these birds are highly vulnerable to exploitation for commercial gains.

## The adoption process

The first step to adopting a Scarlet Macaw is to fill out an application form for adoption. This application form will ask for details about your profession, your experience with birds and also the reason for adoption.

Following this application form, you will be asked to take basics lessons about caring for Scarlet Macaws. These lessons could either be online or offline. You will also be given access to a lot of their educational material that you can refer to after taking the bird home. Many adoption agencies require that you complete a certain number of these basics classes before you are allowed to take a bird home.

After you have completed the required number of training hours, you will be allowed to take a tour of the aviary and the adoption center. That way, you get an idea about all the birds that are available for adoption. There are several cases when people decide that they want a certain bird but end up getting a different species altogether.

The idea is to form a bond with the right bird. Macaws are birds with large personalities. If your personality does not match the bird's personality, you will have a tough time getting your bird to bond with you and actually want to be around you.

The last thing to do would be to visit the bird of your choice frequently. Once you have made up your mind to take a certain Macaw home, you need to let the bird get acquainted with you. You will also learn simple things like handling the bird, feeding him and cleaning the cage up etc. from the experts at the adoption agency.

Sometimes, it may so happen that you set your heart and mind on one bird who just does not seem to be interested. It is natural for that to happen. All you need to do is be patient with the bird and visit him as many times as you can.

When you are ready to take the bird home, most of these adoption centers will pay a visit to your home and will take care of all the little details required to help you get the bird settled into your home.

Now, if you already have pet birds at home, you will be required to present a full veterinary test result of each bird. This helps the agency ensure that the bird they are sending to your home does not have any vulnerability to fatal diseases. There are certain health standards that each of these agencies set for the health of your pet bird.

**Are there any fees involved?**

Most agencies and foundations will charge you an application fee that will include access to educational DVDs, toys and other assistance from the foundation.

You will also have to pay an adoption fee that may go up to $100 or £500 for a Scarlet Macaw. These two separate fees are charged to make sure that you get all the assistance that you need with respect to making a positive start with your Scarlet Macaw.

In addition to that, most agencies charge a rather high fee to ensure that the individuals who are investing in the bird are genuinely interested in having the bird. These fees will ward off people who want to just take the bird home for free with no clue about its care. Of course, you also need to consider the care provided to these birds while they are under the care of the foundation. These fees cover all of that including the medical requirements of your bird. It is also the only source to pay the dedicated staff who take care of these abandoned or rescued birds day in and day out.

From the time you make the application for a Scarlet Macaw, it takes about 6-10 weeks for it to be approved and for the bird to be sent to your home. Most of these centers will also have a probationary period of 90 days during which you will have to keep sending records of how the bird is progressing to them. They will also pay home visits to ensure that the bird is being maintained well without any health issues. If the ambience or the facilities provided to the bird are not good enough, the bird will be taken back with no reimbursement of the adoption fee.

## 3. Buying from a pet store

Getting a Scarlet Macaw from a pet store should be your last option. The reason for this is that these birds do not get the specialized care that they require when they are in a pet store with several other birds and animals, perhaps. However, if you are convinced that a local pet store is known for the quality of Scarlet Macaws that they sell, here are a few things that you need to keep in mind:

- Make sure that the pet store has a license to sell exotic birds. You can check the CITES website for all the details on the license required to buy and sell exotic birds.

- You need to ensure that these birds are being sourced by local breeders. Since importing these birds is illegal, these birds should be bred in captivity. Find out about the breeder that they deal with in detail.

• Check the ambience that the bird is being raised in. A macaw is not a commodity that you pick off the shelf even if it is in a slightly messy environment. These birds hate crammed and dirty places. They will develop behavioral problems and could also be carriers of several diseases when kept in such conditions.

• The pet store should provide a health guarantee for the birds that they sell, especially the exotic ones. Insist on this guarantee because Scarlet Macaws are extremely expensive.

• The bird should look healthy and active. On the other hand, if he or she is lethargic and is afraid of people, it might be a challenge for you to make the bird a part of your family.

• The staff should be interested in the well-being of the bird and should be able to provide you with information regarding the care and maintenance of the bird. If you see that they are negligent and are only trying to make a sale, they have most likely invested almost nothing in the bird's well-being.

A Scarlet Macaw is a wonderful companion, no doubt. However, it is not the easiest bird to have in a household. If you feel like you need to learn a little more about the birds, spend time at pet stores to see how they behave and how demanding they can be.

Adoption centers would be happy to have volunteers who can take care of the birds. This is also a great idea for you to get used to these birds. Their size may be awe-inspiring. However, it is the sheer size of these birds that can make you feel like you are incompetent to take care of them. Handling them, feeding them and even just having them on your shoulder is a lot harder in comparison to a smaller bird.

You can even join local bird groups or dedicated Scarlet Macaw forums to learn more about the bird. Do not be too impulsive about purchasing a Scarlet Macaw. Take your time and only make a decision when you know enough about the bird.

# Chapter 3: Preparing for a Scarlet Macaw

Bringing home a Scarlet Macaw is a lot of responsibility. You need to make sure that you are prepared to bring the bird home before you take the decision. Most people believe that birds are easy to have because they do need to "walk them" or "bathe them".

The truth is that there are several other things that you need to worry about when you bring a Scarlet Macaw home. These birds are extremely sensitive and intelligent. This means that you will have to work a lot harder to keep your bird entertained and happy.

## 1. Exercises to prepare for a pet bird

For at least 6 months prior to bringing your Scarlet Macaw home, it is a good idea to try the following exercises. As mentioned before, there are several small things about having a bird in your home that can actually be quite challenging if you are not prepared. Some of these exercises can seem really gross, but you will know what you are getting into:

- Take big bite of a carrot or any other fruit or vegetable. Chew it well till it is mushy and spit it out on your wall or on the floor anywhere in the house. Then, let it dry until evening. Once it is fully dried, you will have to wipe it down. Do this every day.

- A Scarlet Macaw is expensive. During the last two months of your exercise to prepare for your parrot, go to a supply store and buy everything that you need for a parrot including food and toys. Now, buy your groceries with the remaining money. Is the money that is left over from here good enough to sustain a possible lifestyle that you have created for yourself over the years? If not, how are you going to deal with the extra expense? You cannot make any compromises as far as the requirements of the parrot goes.

- Go to a pet store near your home and place a newspaper at the floor of any large macaw cage. At the end of the day, you will have an idea about the amount of poop you will have to deal with on a daily basis. Now imagine this on your furniture, clothes, the floor etc. occasionally. Is that something you can manage?

- In a gallon box, mix up some feathers, some dried poop and bird seeds or pellets. Now, these things are available in any pet store. Tell them why you need it and they will give it to you, although slightly amused. This mixture should be thrown around the house and cleaned up at least twice every day.

- Although this may sound a little dramatic, it is worth trying. Take a screwdriver and make some holes in your wall. Not all the way through, just to look like it has been gouged by a bird. Now, look at your favorite lamp, imagine it is smashed into pieces. Practice this mental exercise every day.

You need to be well researched about the bird. Read up as many journals and blogs about the Scarlet Macaw as possible. There are certain terms that you need to know such as cloaca, blood feather, papillae, regurgitation etc.

- Sift a cup of flour around the house. Make sure you dust all the surfaces of your home. Clean this up. Repeat this every week at least three times.

- You can get a copy of wild bird sounds that can be timed and played. Play this in the morning for fifteen minutes and at sunset for fifteen minutes. Make sure you play it at full volume.

- Pick out odd things like tissue paper, bottle caps etc. and try to make interesting toys out of them. This is a skill you will have to master as Scarlet Macaws are easily bored with toys and need something new on a daily basis. You can, of course, not splurge on these toys every day. You will soon realize that your bank account is all over the place.

- Keep aside $100 in addition to the supplies that you just bought. This is the medical expense that you can expect. How you are financially placed after putting all this money away?

Besides this, you need to be prepared for things like walking to a grocery store with dry bird poop on your shoulder. They will also gouge holes into your upholstery and your bed sheets. Of course, your bird may also require 15-20 minutes of undivided attention on a daily basis to prevent it from getting bored and developing unwanted health issues.

26

You need to be sure that following this regime for six months has not driven you crazy. When you commit to a Scarlet Macaw, you will have to do all this and a lot more for at least 25 years. That is the average lifespan of these birds.

The idea is not to scare you about Scarlet Macaws. But, this is the truth when you bring a bird home. You could ask any bird owner and they will tell you that everything above is spot on. These exercises will also help you understand whether your entire family is ready to make a commitment to a Scarlet Macaw or not.

## Pros and Cons of having a Scarlet Macaw

Scarlet Macaws have a great personality and make wonderful pets when they are trained right and taught to behave correctly. If you do not have the time for a bird like the macaw which persistently tries to seek your attention, then you may have a tough time.

While there are several pros to having a Scarlet Macaw at home, there are also a few downsides. Let us take a look at both in this section.

### Can Scarlet Macaws have behavioral problems?

Like all macaws, even Scarlet Macaws are big birds not just in size but also in personality. The good news is that research shows us that Scarlet Macaws have fewer behavior problems in comparison to other birds that you can have as pets especially parrots. They are generally noted for a stable temperament. They are also least inclined to have any neurotic problems.

Even if they do exhibit behavioral problems these birds are easier to correct because of their innate curiosity. They do not overreact to threats or any unfamiliar objects in most cases. This is what makes them easier to manage and teach new things to.

### Is chewing an issue?

Yes, this is something that you need to curb right from the word Go! They are not really destructive if trained properly. Since these birds have large beaks, the smallest nibble can cause damage automatically. In comparison to birds like the Hyacinth Macaw, Scarlets tend to be less aggressive when it comes to chewing. You can provide your bird with wooden toys and even set a few rules and guidelines that can restrict the chewing habits to things that you do not mind them getting their beaks on. With a well-trained Scarlet, you do not have to worry about expensive furniture being shredded into pieces.

### Are they noisy?

You bet! Almost all species of macaws can be super-loud and noisy. There are people who claim that they recognize the sounds made by their birds about half a mile away!

But, the good thing is the ability to train these birds to listen to calm down. They will tone down their voices if you can teach it them to. Here is another thing you need to know. If your home is noisy, your bird is going to be noisy. Scarlet Macaws learn and pick up sounds from their household. They also have an instinctive need to keep their sound at par with the sound made by their flock.

If your home is quiet generally, the bird will be the same. This is also because the macaw is quick to understand that his owners prefer to stay quiet.

### Do they love to cuddle?

With Scarlet Macaws, we have discussed it before that they love physical affection. They tend to stay entertained on their own if they have enough toys. However, these birds need you to cuddle with them, speak to them lovingly and have positive interactions on a regular basis. They can be demanding, however, if this behavior isn't corrected soon.

### Is their sexual behavior manageable?

The most noticeable difference in the change in a Macaw's behavior after he or she is sexually mature is that they tend to become noisier and can be a little impatient as well. In comparison to most other pet birds, sexually mature Scarlet Macaws are less radical in that change. However, in comparison to other Macaws, Scarlet Macaws exhibit most change.

In comparison to the male, the females exhibit more changes. They will begin to nest even when there is no male when they are hormonal. But the sexual behavior in these birds is quite easy to manage.

### Do they get along with a family?

Scarlet Macaws are great when it comes to living with many people around them. But, the catch is that they should not feel left out or they shouldn't feel like they are missing out on anything.

If the bird is neglected, he will bite, squawk, or even become aggressive. This is not really a behavioral problem but is a way for your bird to tell you that you need to start paying more attention to him.

## Adolescent behavior in a Macaw

When macaws are young, you need to be really cautious. Though they are fully grown by this time, they tend to be very immature in their behavior, almost like a baby. They will show you their vulnerability and trust. This makes the showcase behaviors like staring into people's eyes, bobbing the head up and down, keeping their crown feathers erect, flipping wings and even vocalizing. They tend to be noisy and make sounds like honking noises and squeals.

When the macaws are younger, they tend to fight with one another. Birds like Hyacinth Macaws even begin to look disheveled and shabby because of the need to be rough. In case of the Scarlet Macaws, their countenance is a lot more demure and dignified.

You will see that these birds become additionally curious in this phase. They will even experiment with behavior patterns. Some days, they become obnoxiously loud and difficult and on the other days they are calm and relaxed. Be careful about nipping and biting as their jaws tend to be really strong.

If you feel like your rather calm and composed scarlet has suddenly gone rowdy, you can blame it on the adolescence. This is when they even tend to bully the other pets at home. Behavior training during this period is mandatory to keep your bird in control. With consistent training, the good macaw behavior does take over quite easily and naturally.

## Can you let them out of the cage?

Of course, you can. And in case of Scarlet Macaws, you should. These birds love to have a lot of floor time. Given the right toys and a secure space, these birds can be very peaceful even when they are out of the cage. They are the least bit destructive and are a delight to have around.

The only challenge you will ever face with a scarlet macaw is that they do not like to be treated as a secondary pet. You have to give them a lot of importance and make them feel like they are a part of your family too.

## 2. Housing the Scarlet Macaw

Housing a Scarlet Macaw is a challenge owing to the sheer size of the bird. It isn't enough to just build a cage for the bird and leave him there. There are several factors that you need to consider in order to keep the bird comfortable in your home:

• The depth of the tail and the wingspan: Your Scarlet Macaw should be able to stretch in the cage easily. The wingspan of the bird is about 3-4 feet in length on an average. The minimum size of the cage should be such that your bird is able to spread his wings without touching the sides of the cage. The tail is also long, so you have to make sure that it does not get entangled in the bars of the cage.

The minimum size requirement for a Scarlet Macaw cage is a depth of 30 inches, height of 60-72 inches and a width of 48 inches. If you are able to get a cage that actually allows your bird to fly, it is called a true flight cage. This would ideally be about twice the size of the dimensions mentioned above.

In case of large macaws, the most important factor is the depth. Most breeders recommend that the deeper the cage, the better it is for the bird, although it makes it hard to handle the bird and reach out. The key to keeping your bird in a deep cage is to train them well to step up.

### a. Strong beaks need strong cages

A fully grown Scarlet Macaw can easily chew his way through the cage if the bars are not sturdy enough. There are several kinds of cages made from different material that you will find at pet stores. The best option for a bird like the Scarlet Macaw is a stainless steel one.

Most Scarlet Macaw breeders will tell you that material is certainly important. But, what you need to focus on more is the construction of the cage. If you are certain that the cage is welded properly, then you can be sure of your bird's safety. Another type of construction is square tubing which is sturdier. However, it is harder to clean.

The ideal diameter of the bar is about ¼ inch and the distance between them should be between ½ to 2 inches. In case of a 2 inch spacing between the bar, you will be able to see the bird better. It also helps the bird climb the cage easily. However, if the spacing is too much, it may lead to the tail getting entangled and will also reduce the grip that your bird gets to climb and stay active enough during their time inside the cage.

On the other hand, if you are able to provide your bird with a cage that is large enough, he is less likely to want to chew. He will stay entertained and will be a lot easier for you to train to behave well, too.

**b.Keeping them busy**
The cage ought to be the bird's haven. If he does not enjoy going back into the cage, chances are that he will fuss around to go back in after being trained to step up or step out.

For this, you need to give the bird a lot of toys that he can chew on, climb and just play with. There are several things like soft wood that you can give your bird to also keep the beak in good condition.

At the same time, make sure that the cage does not get overcrowded. If your bird is constantly hitting his head against the toys, it is an indication that there are too many toys. If a bird as large as the Scarlet Macaw is able to hide behind these toys, it is also a sign that you need to go easy on the toys. Lastly, the bird needing to actually walk through a maze of toys to get to his food is also an indication that you have gone overboard with the number of toys in the cage.

**c. Be prepared for a big mess**
A bird as big as a Scarlet Macaw is bound to make a big mess. So, make sure that the cage floor is made of material that is easy to clean up. It doesn't matter if it is an indoor or outdoor cage, being easy to clean is the key. This also ensures that your birds are in the pink of their health at all times.

Now, surfaces like plastic, tile and concrete are great and are really easy to clean. The best option is chair mats made of plastic that are normally used on office chairs. They cannot be torn and eaten by the bird. Also, there is no risk of the bird hurting themselves on a hard surface.

If you have an aviary, it is best that you include a drain in it. The more birds you have, the more the mess. The drain will also make it easier when you wash the aviary once every 15-20 days.

**d. Placing the perches in the cage**
The toes of your Scarlet Macaws stay in shape and stay protected when you have proper perches in the cage. You can get a good variety of these perches in pet stores. You need to make sure that your bird can get all of his toes around the perch for him to benefit from it. The ideal size of a

perch is up to 2 inches in diameter. You can also get flat perches that will serve as resting perches.

You may choose to hang these perches vertically as well. That makes for a fun activity for your macaw. Watch as they hang on to the perch and climb. The best material for these perches is soft wood that is also safe for the birds to chew on.

### e. Food and water containers

The Scarlet Macaw is a large bird. So, it is necessary for you to provide him with containers that are large and sturdy enough to eat from. Some owners actually use dog dishes made from stainless steel. All you need is material that is easy to clean and sturdy. The ideal size for the food and water containers of scarlets is 3 inches in depth and about 8 inches in diameter.

You can even make feeding time fun by adding foraging boxes near the food and water containers. They can even be card board boxes that you place food in and make the birds work for it. This box can be changed everyday in case your bird begins to chew on it! This should be for special foods only. So add a treat or your bird's favorite food. The harder you make it for them to access the food, the longer they will stay entertained!

### f. Tips about outdoor aviaries

If you have the space for it, the outdoor aviary is the best option for your bird. These enclosures are large and spacious. They also ensure that your bird has complete access to sunlight.

If you decide to have an outdoor aviary for your Scarlet Macaws, make sure you have enough place for them to cool off and rest. This includes areas that are shaded and covered. You can even add water misters to make the outdoor aviary more comfortable for your bird.

When you have an outdoor aviary, you also have several choices before you. You may choose to make this an aviary that houses birds of many species. You can also make this a recreational area where your birds can fly around and get enough exercise until they are properly trained.

If you choose the latter, make sure that you take precautions to keep your birds safe from predators and also theft. The first thing you need to do is install a secure door that you will lock any time you leave the birds unsupervised. You can also install fences that will keep your bird safe from the most common predators.

If you choose the former, you will also have to consider the complications of housing several species together. The Scarlet Macaw should be fine with most large macaws. The only birds you will want to keep separately are Hyacinth Macaws as their diet is very specific. You do not want them to eat what is not meant for them or lose out on their food.

It is necessary that you get your birds to spend a lot of time playing outside the cage after they have been trained. This gives them a neutral ground where they can get along with one another. The Scarlet Macaw is a highly dignified bird that is compatible with most other species. However, you must never assume and ensure that you follow the right methods of introduction as mentioned in this book.

It is only through trial and error that you can make a compatible flock of birds in your home. You need to move single birds or groups of birds around until you have a group that interacts peacefully.

Housing your Scarlet Macaw is the most important factor in ensuring a healthy bird. It is bets that you arrange for an enclosure for your bird before you actually bring him home.

If you wish to, you can even buy easy to assemble aviaries and cages for an outdoor set up. For indoor housing, make sure you scout around till you find a cage that is big enough and strong enough to house your powerful scarlet macaw. There are several other options such as ordering enclosures online after discussions with your vet or other experienced Scarlet owners.

g. **Cage maintenance**
It is not enough that you have a beautiful bird cage in your home. You need to make sure that you take good care of this cage and keep it clean to ensure good health of the bird. Of course, no one would want to have a smelly bird cage in their room. There are different frequencies of cleaning for each part of the cage. This is your guide to proper bird cage maintenance:

- **Everyday cleaning:** You will have to spend a few minutes each day examining the cage and making sure that it is in good condition. On a daily basis, you will have to replace the substrate that you have placed on the floor of the cage. You will also have to make sure that the food and water bowls are cleaned and the contents are changed every single day.

If you notice any toy with a lot of poop on it, it will have to be cleaned immediately. In case of food that has been spilled, fruits and vegetables should not be allowed to stay on for more than one hour in the cage. Eating a small piece of rotting fruit or vegetable can cause GI tract infections almost immediately.

- **Fortnightly cleaning:** Every 15 days, a complete wipe down of the cage is necessary. Using any antibacterial cleaner that you can get in any pet store, wipe the floor and the bars of the cage. Dirty toys can also be wiped with the same liquid. This cleaning practice must be followed regularly to reduce the breeding grounds for microbes and thus reduce the chances of infection. If the cage is damp, remove the bird from the cage and allow the cage to dry naturally in the sun for a few minutes before replacing the bird.

- **Monthly cleaning:** Whether you have an aviary or just a single cage, this monthly thorough cleaning is a must. First, you need to place the bird in a temporary cage or enclosure. Then, all the accessories including the chains that are used to hold these toys up should be removed and soaked in an antibacterial solution or even mild soap water.

The cage should be cleaned thoroughly. First, any dried feces or debris should be scraped out. Following this, the cage should be washed completely using soapy water. For those who prefer natural cleaning agents, diluted vinegar is a great option.

Make sure that the toys and the cage are rinsed thoroughly to remove any traces of soap. After that, you can allow them to dry in the sun before you replace them in the cage. You will let the bird into the cage only after everything is fully dry.

This cleaning schedule is quite easy to follow and is usually preferred by most bird owners. You will have a clean and hygienic cage that is free from disease causing microbes. In addition to that, keeping an indoor cage clean is a must to keep your family healthy as well.

# 3. Bird proofing your home

A human home is seldom bird friendly. Our homes consist of glass items, Teflon coated pans and of course AC vents that seem normal and mundane to us. These simple household items can be hazardous to your bird and it is necessary for you to take the following measure to bird proof your home:

- Avoid using Teflon coated pans. These pans release certain fumes that can be fatal for a Scarlet Macaw or any other bird for that matter. If you cannot eliminate Teflon pans, you need to at least ensure that the housing area of the bird is away from the kitchen.

- Breakable items should be kept out of the flight path of your bird. It is best to avoid them altogether as they may cause serious accidents that you will most certainly regret. You can keep these delicate items in areas of the house that the bird will most likely not access.

- Lead weights on curtains and blinds should be removed as lead poisoning occurs quite easily when the bird comes in contact with it.

- Keep loose wires out of the way. Bird tend to tug at any loose wire and may get electrocuted in the process.

- Install a door to the kitchen. The kitchen has several hot items like pans, stove tops etc that can cause serious burns to your bird if he sits on them unknowingly. If not, you can get special covers for these surfaces quite easily.

- Ceiling fans should be kept off whenever the bird is out of the cage. You must also avoid switching on table fan when the bird is flying around the house.

- Never keep plain glass windows spotlessly clean. Mark them by placing items like pots at the window sill. You can even add stickers to these clean glass surfaces to ensure that the birds do not flu right into them and suffer from injuries.

- The cage should be kept away from hard surfaces. If you have a baby bird, he may attempt to fly and fall several times in the process. A fall on a hard cement floor can be fatal to the bird.

- Keep the cage away from the air conditioner or the radiator. Cold or hot emissions from these machines can cause several health problems in Scarlet Macaws. Keep the cage in an area of the house that is extremely cosy.

Once you have a bird in your home, you will always have to make sure that they doors and windows are shut. Whenever you put the bird back in the cage, lock the door properly. Also be careful when you open and close the door. If your bird is let out loose most of the time, slamming the door can lead to a trapped bird with multiple injuries. Lastly, be prepared to make changes as per the personality of your bird. All you need to remember is that any health risk should be out of the way entirely.

## 4. Preparing the family for the Scarlet Macaw

When you are bringing a Scarlet Macaw home, it is natural for the family to be just as excited as you to welcome home a new member of the family. However, the Scarlet Macaw isn't just any pet bird, it is a sizeable bird with great mandible power and several special requirements.

This bird is also highly sensitive and will analyze every situation in your home before becoming a part of the household. So, you need to lay a few ground rules to prepare your family for the bird as well:

- The bird will not be disturbed during its initial days in your home. This includes no teasing, no bringing friends over to see the bird, no parties, no loud music and even no talking to the bird. That way, you can establish a sense of security with the new members.

- One must never stick their finger into the cage even for fun. These birds will bite when threatened. And, the bite will be powerful enough to rip a person's finger tip off.

- The responsibilities of feeding the bird will be divided. Initially, the other family members can be accompanied by the person whose bird it is. Then, they will have to do this on their own. Spending time feeding the bird, especially, helps the bird know all the members of the family and associate them with food which is quite positive. Birds are not threatened by their family or their flock as long as they are part of the daily routine.

- Everybody will learn about the Scarlet Macaw in complete detail. They can also attend the basics training class with you if you are adopting your bird.

- No one will tease the bird with large and colorful objects like balls or toys. These things make the bird look at you like a predator and will withdraw himself from you. They will also make the bird susceptible to behavior issues if repeated persistently.

- Whoever leaves the house last will check all the doors and windows and will make sure that they cage is closed. If there are any other additional measures like separating the household pets, it should be done by this person. The person leaving the house last is responsible for taking all the safety measures with respect to the bird who will be left alone all day.

- Only one person in the house will take the responsibility of training the bird. If you use multiple methods or cues, the bird will simply get confused and will not respond to training effectively. This is usually done by the person who is closest to the bird or by someone who has better experience with training and caring for birds.

- Do not encourage the household pets to attack the cage even for fun. Cats or dogs are natural predators who may cause a lot of harm to your Scarlet Macaw. In case of this large bird, even vice versa is possible, considering the size and the power of this bird.

When you bring a Scarlet Macaw home, you need to understand that you are bringing home a highly evolved life form. They understand the slightest changes in their ambience. It is the job of the entire family to ensure that the bird feels comfortable in the house and feels like a part of the flock.

Your family should be educated about the needs of Scarlet Macaws to make sure that they are alert in case of any emergency. If nothing else, you need to make sure that they know how to provide first aid for common accidents like bleeding and broken feathers.

The whole family should be aware of where the first aid box is placed and where the supplies for the birds are located. They should also have the number of the vet fed into their phones. This way, you are all on the same page as far as first aid and emergency care is concerned.

The larger the flock, the happier a Scarlet Macaw is. So make sure your family can be the ideal and most loving flock imaginable.

# Chapter 4: Caring for your Scarlet Macaw

There are several things that you will have to do for your Scarlet Macaw from the time you bring one home. These affectionate, loving birds can be quite a handful if they are not given the time that they require. You also have to make sure that your bird gets the right food and nutrition to keep them in the best condition.

This chapter will take you in detail through all the care requirements of the Scarlet Macaw from the time you bring the bird into your home.

## 1. Helping the Bird Settle In

The first day of the bird in your home can be very hard on him or her. The transition from the breeders' or the adoption center to your home can be very strenuous. Scarlet Macaws like any other bird from the family of parrots dislike change and will be withdrawn and a little scared for the first few days. Here are a few tips to make this transition easy for your beloved new pet:

- When you are driving the bird home from the adoption center or from the breeders, keep your car quiet. Roll the windows up, set the air conditioner up to room temperature and place the cage of the bird in such a way that there are no bumps or movements. If your home is far away from the breeders' make sure that you stop frequently to let the bird relax. Do not talk to the bird or play loud music during the drive.

- Make sure that the housing for your bird is set up before you bring him home. Then, just place the door of the transfer cage towards the door of the bird's new home and wait for him to walk in.

- Make plenty of fresh water and food available to the bird. In case your bird has been on a seed diet at the breeders' do not try to change it right away. You can make the changes after the bird is accustomed to the new environment. In the meanwhile, it is alright to introduce a few fruits and fresh vegetables to your bird and see how he responds.

- The cardinal rule on day one is to leave the bird alone. Let him try to understand his new surroundings first. He will most probably not

get on with your chores. Make sure your bird is able to see you. .en you enter the room that the bird is placed in just greet him with a ilo and say goodbye when you leave the room. This should be practiced y everyone in the family so that the bird gets acquainted with the voice.

For the first few days, do not allow anyone else to feed the bird. This should be done by the person who got the bird home. When your bird forms a bond with you, it is safer to introduce him to the other members in your family.

Lastly, the first few days are very crucial to determine if your bird is showing signs of any behavioral or physical problems. So, observe the bird carefully. If you see that there is any change from what is normal such as too much water consumption, lack of energy, staggering while walking, heavy breathing, lack of appetite or even excessive aggression, it might be a good idea to consult the vet. That way, any problem can be fixed in the initial stages so that you can enjoy the rest of your journey with your Scarlet Macaw.

### b. Introducing the bird to other pets
If you have a home with multiple pets, then introducing a new bird is a little tricky. The Scarlet Macaw is a large bird, so when you are introducing him to your pets, you need to remember that they are both equally dangerous to each other. The mandible power of the Scarlet Macaw can injure your pet dog and cat quite badly. That is why you need to be extremely cautious when making the introductions.

### Scarlet Macaws, Cats and Dogs

Cats and dogs are predators by the natural order. That already makes them a threat to your Scarlet Macaw irrespective of how sweet and friendly they are towards people.

During the first few days, allow the bird to become aware of the presence of the other animal. Let him watch and observe your pet cat or dog. There must be no surprises later on. Just make sure that your dog or cat does not approach the cage while you are away. Your cat, especially, should not be allowed to climb over the cage.

When the bird seems settled in, it is time for the introductions. While keeping the bird in the cage, you will let the dog or cat around it. Let them sniff and explore. If your dog begins to bark or if your cat becomes aggressive, separate them instantly.

Now, keep doing this until your dog or cat is used to the bird. That will make them ignore the new member of the family even when in the same room. When you have reached this stage, it may be safe to let the bird out and interact with the pets.

You can take this liberty only when your dog or cat has been trained well to heel. When these animals are trained, the risk to the bird is reduced to a large extent as you will be able to control your cat or dog even if they just get too excited.

If you see that your pet cat or dog is chasing the bird around, you must put the bird back in the cage. In case your bird is not hand trained, wrap a towel around his body and your hands while handling him.

In any case, it is never advisable to leave the bird alone with your pets. While they may seem to get along with each other perfectly well in your presence, do not take any risks.

A dog can seriously harm the Scarlet Macaw with a simple friendly nibble. At the same time, your Scarlet Macaw can rip the dog's ear right off when provoked. As for cats, the biggest threat is the saliva of the cat which is poisonous for a Scarlet Macaw.

Remember that you are dealing with highly instinctive creatures. You can never be sure of when their instinctive behavior will kick in. So, it is best that you let them interact in your presence. In case there are any signs of aggression, it is best to keep your Scarlet Macaw confined in the presence of the cat or the dog.

## Scarlet Macaws and other pet birds

The first step to introducing new birds is to have the bird quarantined for 30 days at least. This gives you enough time to observe the bird for any signs of infection that could be contagious. To quarantine the new bird, you need to keep him or her in a separate cage, in a separate room. Birds will get acquainted with one another thanks to their loud calls. So, you can expect your pet birds to be ready for a new member during the introduction.

It is never a good idea to place birds of different sizes in the same cage. The larger bird might become more dominating, putting the smaller bird at great risk. If you have an aviary with birds about the same size as the Scarlet Macaws such as the Cockatoo, you could keep them together.

41

However, there is no guarantee that your birds will be friendly with each other and will take to each other's company.

During the actual introduction, you will introduce your Scarlet Macaw to the least dominant bird in the flock. You can first start by placing them in separate cages side by side. You can also get a new cage that they both can be placed in, in order to reduce territorial behavior. If the birds just mind their own business and do not attack one another, you can consider it a successful introduction. You can progress to the more dominant birds in the same fashion.

These introductions will only happen in your presence so that you can observe the behavior of the birds. When you are introducing the more dominant birds to your Scarlet Macaw, it is best to do it in a more open space like the living room. This gives the bird ample room to run away or fly away if there is any sign of aggression from the other one.

After you are certain that these individual introductions went well, you can place the bird in the aviary. Watch the reaction of the other birds carefully. If you notice that one of them retreats completely, it is a sign that he or she is not happy with the new member in the group. On the other hand, if you see your Scarlet Macaw being chased around the cage, he could be in danger of attacks and wounds.

Birds may get along with no traces of jealousy or dominance at times. But if this does not happen in your home despite several attempts, it is not a matter of great disappointment. Sometimes, birds may just not get along with one another. That is when you place them in separate cages and leave them alone.

This ensures that no bird is harmed unnecessarily. You will also prevent a great deal of stress that the bird may go through when he is introduced to another bird who is so hostile or even aggressive in some cases.

## 2. Feeding a Scarlet Macaw

Feeding exotic birds can be quite challenging as you need to make their diet as close to their natural foods as possible. With the Scarlet Macaw, it is true that the birds require a high fat diet. However, even with this diet, there is a certain limit to the fat that you can provide to your bird. Excessive fat can make the bird obese, putting a lot of pressure on the internal organs and also making the bird lethargic. It also affects the metabolism of nutrients like calcium.

In the wild, these birds mostly eat several types of nuts and fruits. They also include vegetables in their diet. But, a large part of the bird's diet consists of palm nuts. Of course, sourcing these foods can be quite difficult and you will have to make modifications as required.

It is a good idea to make a mixture of nuts along with the shells to give your Scarlet Macaw. This can contain almonds, filberts, Brazil nuts, walnuts, pecans and Macadamia nuts. Macadamia nuts should form the large part of the mixture.

A small serving of these mixed nuts can be given to the bird everyday. They are very nutritious, free from cholesterol and give the bird the necessary amount of Vitamin A, Calcium, Phosphorous, Niacin, fiber and protein. Keeping the shell on also allows them to condition their beaks and is a great source of entertainment for the bird.

You will have to keep the regular pellets and the nuts in separate bowls. While pellets do not entirely constitute a balanced diet for the birds, they are certainly a better option than seeds. Of course, these foods do not spoil easily and can be left in the cage all day long.

You must also include fresh produce like fruits and vegetables in the diet of your bird. These soft foods can be given to the bird at about mid-morning. Allow the bird to eat this for a while and when he turns away from it, clean out the food immediately. This food should not be left in the cage for too long.

You need to maintain a certain routine with feeding your bird. The first thing in the morning should be providing the pellets and the nuts. Clean the bowls from the previous day, allow them to dry and add fresh food and water every morning, even if it means wasting a little of the previous day's food. This keeps the cage clean and free from infections of any kind.

Fresh produce will improve the health of your bird. They make the immune system stronger, provide the birds with necessary minerals and vitamins and will also give them a good attitude because they are happy.

Learn as much about bird nutrition as you possibly can when you bring a Scarlet Macaw home. This will allow you to make changes in the diet as required and keep the food bowl interesting for the bird.

Fruits like watermelon are great for your Scarlet Macaw. These fruits are a wonderful source of Vitamin A, B6 and Vitamin C that maintain the eye health of the bird, fight infections, help curb feather picking in birds and even keep the body free from toxins and free radicles.

Some fruits and vegetables that you can give your bird everyday include:

- Papaya
- Cantaloupe
- Mango
- Honeydew melon
- Kiwi
- Banana
- Blueberry
- Grapefruit
- Strawberry
- Oranges
- Peaches
- Watermelon
- Pomegranate
- Beets
- Pea pods
- Green beans
- Star fruits
- Carrots
- Broccoli
- Green Peppers
- Zucchini
- Yams
- Radish
- Cooked Beans

Whenever you are giving your bird any fruits that contain a pit, make sure it is removed. Even seeds from fruits like apples may have a few toxins that can harm the bird. To be safe, remove the seeds from all fruits while feeding your Scarlet Macaw. Never give your bird Avocados as they are toxic to them.

Never give your bird any foods that contain preservatives, added salts or sugars. Choose organically grown foods that are not processed.

If your bird was used to a seed based diet with the breeders, you need to slowly make a transition by adding pellets to the seeds and then increasing the quantity of the pellets gradually. Seeds will make the birds obese and have very little nutritional value.

Since your birds in captivity do not have the joy of foraging, you can make eating time more fun for them by giving them half a cantaloupe or watermelon instead of cutting it into pieces. You can also give them corn on the cob so they can pick and eat from it. This keeps them mentally well stimulated and will make them look forward to eating sessions.

Now, it is possible that your Scarlet Macaw will be picky when it comes to the natural fresh produce. It is a good idea to give the bird a range of foods over a few days to see what he likes and what he doesn't. It is best to give the bird the foods that he enjoys. This is because he will not only not eat the food but will also pick at it, fling it around and make a massive mess.

You will also need to observe the amount of food the bird eats and restrict the serving size accordingly. Leaving food in the bowl will eventually lead to a big mess. In case of supplements in the food, you must never add any on your own, unless recommended by the vet. Some vitamins like Vitamin D can actually harm your bird when given in excess. Even if the supplement is "parrot safe" as per the boxes, it will become unsafe if your bird does not require any additional supplement. As we have seen before, Scarlet Macaws have a very wide range of foods that they consume in the wild. So, you need to make sure that the same variety is available to the birds even when you are raising them as pets. This is to make sure that they do not get bored of certain foods and refuse to eat them.

The core diet of the bird should consist of bird pellets without any color, dry bird mix that is very high in quality and organic elements. You can even look for bird mix that is organic or all natural. One thing that you need to avoid giving your bird is fortified foods that really do not help as much as you would imagine. In fact, these foods can do more harm than good to your bird. The solution to make sure that your bird gets all the nutrients he requires is to get organic bird mix and then add a good quality supplement as recommended by a vet.

Here is a list of the ideal food that you must include in your Scarlet Macaw's diet:

**Pellets:** The concept of feeding birds pellets became quite popular in the 90s and several brands began to manufacture pellets on a large scale. This even led to some pellets that contained harmful additives or even a poor balance of nutrients. This is why you should be very particular about the brand that you choose. One of the most popular brands for bird pellets is Harrison. It is a formulated pellet that you can give your bird without the risk of any chances of malnutrition. In any case, it is best to consult your avian vet before deciding upon the pellet that you give your bird.

With formulated pellets, you need to make sure that you do not give your bird an overdose of vitamin C as it can cause an Iron overload disease. Vitamin C increases the body's ability to absorb iron. Therefore be very cautious when you are giving your bird fruits like orange when he is already on a fortified pellet diet.

**Base diet mix:** If you are one of those bird owners who does not like the idea of giving your bird pellets, then there are diet mixes from companies like Lafaber and Dr. Harvey's. They are certainly the best as they do not contain any additives that are seen in most commercially available bird diet mixes.

These pre-mixed foods consist of herbs, vegetables and fruits (dried) and even some avian super foods like bee pollen. These foods are very nutritious and can give your Scarlet Macaw the variety that is needed in their diet.

However, there is one concern with commercially available foods which makes it a wiser choice to mix the foods yourself. All the dried produce that is available in these commercially prepared foods are sulphureted, making it harmful for your bird when given excessively. It is a better idea to buy grains, seeds and fresh produce and mix them up. All you need is a little creativity in order to give your bird optimum nutrition.

All you have to do is remember that seeds need to be provided in moderation to your birds. In addition to that, seeds should be fresh and clean.

### a. Foods that you can mix in your bird's diet:

- The seeds that you can use include pumpkin seeds, fennel seeds, safflower seeds and sunflower seeds.
- Nuts that are best suited for Scarlet Macaws are cashews, brazil nuts, macadamia nuts, pine nuts, walnuts, almonds and filberts.
- There are several greens, fruits and vegetables that can be included in the diet such as papaya, corn, soy beans, mangoes, pears, peaches, apple, carrot, pineapple, apricots, broccoli, thyme, bell peppers, celery, spinach, raspberries and basil.

46

Remember that avocados can be poisonous for your bird and must never be included in the diet. If you want to provide your bird with raisins, it should be given in small quantities only in order for your bird to get maximum benefits.

In general, all macaws need to have a higher level of fat in their diet. This can be ensured to your bird by giving them nuts as an integral part of their diet. As for the fruits and vegetables, you can try a large variety for your bird. You will see that they will pick their likes and dislikes.

### b. Other sources of foods

- Baby food: Human baby food along with fresh fruits and vegetables makes a great base mix for your bird.
- Dried produce: In case you are unable to source fresh produce, you can give your bird dried vegetables and fruits. In fact, birds enjoy the fact that these foods are crunchy. You also have the option of soaking these foods in warm water. This, it is believed, reminds the birds of the regurgitated foods given to them by parents which is also moist and warm. These foods help birds progress from seeds to a healthier diet option.
- You need to make sure that any food that you are giving your bird has no artificial coloring. This is usually done to make foods visually more attractive and can be harmful in terms of nutrition. The other thing to avoid is sulfur dioxide. Check the labels thoroughly to ensure that your foods do not have any traces of this chemical. It may make your bird hyper active, can increase aggressive behavior and can even lead to feather plucking or shedding. Allergic reactions to these additives can have mild to severe symptoms that you need to watch out for.

The most convenient food option for Scarlet Macaws is sprouted seeds. This is when you do not have time to prepare the base mix with veggies, seeds etc. An equal portion of these sprouted seeds can be very nutritious. In addition to that, birds simply love sprouted seeds and they are a great way to introduce greens to your bird.

### c. Foods that should be given in moderation

- Any veggies that contain many oxalates should be given to the Scarlet Macaw in moderation. This includes bok choy, spinach and even chard. This is because the absorption of calcium is compromised with these foods.
- Fruits that contain too much sugar must be avoided entirely.

- Any food that is 100% cooked, including beans, pasta or grains. These foods tend to have more calories and are also high in phosphorous. This puts your bird at the risk of becoming obese.
- Seeds should be provided occasionally or as treats, most preferably. This is because they have very little nutritional value and are high in fats.

**d. Foods that you should avoid:**
- Caffeine
- Chocolate
- Alcohol
- Pits of fruits like apricots, plums, peaches and nectarines. This leads to vomiting or even coma as these pits contain enzyme inhibitors.
- Green potatoes, tomato leaves, eggplant. These foods contain poisonous alkaloids. They may lead to diarrhea, vomiting and even difficulty in breathing.
- Raw beans should never be given to macaws as it hampers their protein metabolism. In addition to that, it also contains other toxins that can harm the bird. Giving your bird cooked beans occasionally is a better option.
- Nutmeg is a complete no as it contains myristicin which makes your bird nauseous and dizzy. It can also cause vomiting in birds immediately after consumption.
- Rhubarb leaves are extremely toxic to birds. They contain an intestinal irritant, oxalic acid. If your bird consumes large doses of this compound, it could be lethal.
- Do not allow your bird to ingest tobacco fumes or eat the leaves. This leads to seizures, diarrhea and more severe symptoms. Basically, if you are a smoker, you will want to keep your bird as far away from the smoking area of your home as possible.

Scarlet Macaws are large birds who need good nutrition and good portions of the right nutrients in order for them to thrive. If you are uncertain about what you must give your bird, you may even consult your vet or an experienced Scarlet Macaw owner. But, never assume that what is good for you must be good for the bird. They have different requirements in terms of diet and you need to be careful about maintaining a balance of all the nutrients that they need.

# 3. Finding the perfect vet

Healthcare is the most important thing for your bird. If you do not have the assistance of a good avian vet, you will find it challenging to ensure that your bird gets the best medical aid possible. Annual checkups with an avian vet can be life saving for your bird in many cases.

Vets that treat regular pets like cats and dogs will not be able to help your bird with specific illnesses like PDD or PBFD that we will discuss in the following chapters.

You will have to look for an avian vet who specializes in treating exotic birds.

The first step is to locate an avian vet who is near you. You can look up the website of the Association of Avian Vets to search for certified vets location-wise. If that does not help you find a vet close to your home, you can even enquire at the office of vets who treat other pets or in the pet supply store. Your breeder will be able to help you the best.

Avian vets hold a degree in veterinary studies just like the other vets. However, they specialize in treating birds and a major part of their practice consists of working with birds and diseases related to exotic birds.

In case of the Scarlet Macaw, it is a good idea to look for an Avian vet who is a member of the Association of Avian vets.

**What is the Association of Avian Vets?**

This organization was founded in the year 1980 with the intention of improving the practices of avian medicine. The members of this group comprise mostly of private veterinarians, veterinarians working for zoos, students of veterinary sciences as well as technicians in the field of avian medicine.

The advantage with a vet who is a part of this organization is that he will be up to date with all the latest trends and practices in the field of avian medicine. Through regular conferences and online educational material, the AAV reaches out to all its members with the necessary information to upgrade their practice.

The goal of the AAV is to make sure that the veterinarians associated with it become more competent. If you have found a vet who is a member of the AAV, credibility is something that you do not have to worry about.

With the AAV, the idea of promoting these birds as companions and valuable possessions is of utmost importance. This ensures that the vets associated with this organization will be sensitive towards your beloved pet and will make sure that they get the best services available.

Even for bird owners, the AAV works hard to help them understand how important veterinary care is for the well-being of their bird. They are encouraged to look for only qualified vets. With the massive backing of this organization, the good news is that the number of these vets is fast growing. Therefore, it is easier to find qualified avian vets who can take good care of exotic birds these days.

**Learn more about your avian vet**

When you have finally located a good avian vet, the next step is to make sure that they are the right people to entrust your bird with. Even if a vet is not associated with the AAV the confidence with which he or she answers the following questions will help you decide if you want to be associated with them in the long run or not.

- **How many years have you been treating birds for?** As you know, expertise comes with experience. If your vet has a good background with treating birds, you can be certain that your birds are in safe hands.

- **Are you familiar with Scarlet Macaws?** New world parrots can be very different from old world parrots. Of course, parrots have a totally different response to certain treatments in comparison to other birds. So, if you are looking for a vet for your Scarlet Macaw, the best thing to do would be to look for someone with enough experience with this species.

- **Do you have your own pet birds?** Anyone who has their own pet will be sensitive to the bond that you share with your bird and will be available for most emergencies without any complaints. These people are also likely to understand the body language of your bird and will be able to pick up on even the most subtle signs of illnesses that can help in diagnosing the health issue.

- **Are emergency services available?** If your vet has a pet hospital with an emergency room, it is the best option for you. You must also ask for after hours help in case your bird has any emergency. If your vet is not able to provide this service himself, he will be able to suggest other facilities that can be of great help to you.

- **Will you make house calls?** Sometimes the bird may be too sick to travel with you to the vet. In case of accidents resulting in skull or leg fractures, you must not even move the bird to keep the condition from getting worse. Your vet should be willing to make house calls or must be able to send one of his staff members at the very least.

- **How many checkups will be required in a year?** A good vet will suggest that you get at least one checkup each year to ensure that your bird is in good health. Anyone who is not too concerned about the annual checkup is not genuinely interested in the well-being of your bird.

The tone of your vet and the confidence with which he or she answers these questions will help you understand how genuine they are in their interests to treat your bird. If they seem too standoffish and unpleasant, you can always move on to other vets who will be happy to have you.

While you are at it, observe the way the vet interacts with your birds and other patients of his. A warm and welcoming vet will be able to make this experience less stressful for the birds. He should be confident in holding and handling the bird. If the examinations take place with the birds in the cage in all cases, you are possibly not in the right hands.

Every examination must be thorough and complete. If your vet is seeing one patient every 15 minutes then you can be sure that this is an extremely commercial practice that will not pay close attention to your beloved pet.

Some of these avian vets may treat other pets as well. However, the frequency of the number of feathered patients should be high. If an individual claims to be an avian vet but you only see one bird or two of them over the day, he is probably not best suited for your Scarlet Macaw.

The staff will also say a lot about the facility. They should be familiar with your bird's type. If they are well trained professionals, they will also not have any trouble handling the bird. Watch the way they interact with other pets and pet parents. Are they cheerful? Or are they just interested in getting them in line for the appointments?

Take a good look around the facility. Is it well maintained and sterilized? If they have in-patient services, do each of the birds have their own housing areas. If yes, how are these housing areas maintained. Remember, the pet hospital can be a big source of germs and microbes that will infect your bird. They should also have facilities like gram scales, updated instruments and well maintained equipment.

When you are convinced about the person that you have approached, you can assign them with the role of being the caretaker of your bird's health.

While you are at it, you can even ask about the insurance policies available for pet birds. Some of them will cover most medical expenses in case of an emergency and will also be able to provide third party liability in case of any damage caused by your bird to another person's property. Your vet will be associated with certain health insurance companies that can help you take care of all the medical expenses with respect to your bird.

Usually, these insurance policies have a premium of $100-250 or £50 to 100 depending upon the cover that you are looking at. However they are worth the investment as you will be able to get a lot of support when your bird requires any emergency care or assistance. Last minute expenses can be very stressful if your bird does not have insurance.

In addition to that, insurance will come in very handy when you are travelling with your bird. Most airlines insist that your bird be insured before taking them on board. For the medical expenses, you also have the option of opening a savings account that you can set aside some money in on a monthly basis to help in case of an emergency.

## 4. Keeping the Scarlet Macaw entertained

This is actually an important part of the care that you provide for your Scarlet Macaw. Along with good food and healthcare, you need to ensure that your Scarlet Macaw is getting ample mental stimulation to avoid any behavioral issues like feather plucking. They may also display attention seeking behavior like screaming or biting if you fail to keep them well entertained.

Here are a few tips to help you keep the bird mentally stimulated. You could even come up with other activities along the way as you get to know your feathered friend's preferences and dislikes:

- Make sure that your bird has a large enough cage that he can move around freely in. If the place is too congested and small, he will just stay on the perch and will become highly inactive.

- Scarlet Macaws are highly social creatures. If you keep your bird in a quiet room that is completely away from the daily activities in your household, he will demand attention. Instead, make sure that this room is quiet but is facing the room with maximum activity, such as the living room, to help observe and stay alert at all times.

- You can introduce a companion to your bird or just buy the macaws in pairs. This works wonderfully as it keeps your bird engaged and will make him demand for your time and attention a lot less than you expect. If you are introducing the new companion, make sure you follow all the steps mentioned above to keep your bird and the new bird safe.

- Give your macaw a lot of free time. They cannot spend the whole day confined in the cage now, can they? It is advised that you give your parrot at least two hours outside the cage every day. If you have a play top cage, it will become your bird's favorite resting spot. You can even get a large parrot gym that will allow your parrot to climb and perform several acrobatics for you.

- Bring home as many bird toys as you can. You have several colors, sizes and shapes of toys that your macaw will fall in love with. Keep recycling the toys instead of throwing everything in at once. That will help you keep his interest in these toys for a longer time. Also, try homemade toys like wrapping a few seeds in paper, rolling it up into a ball and placing it in the cage. See the frenzy with which your bird will attack that ball of paper.

- Include your bird in all celebrations. If you are celebrating a birthday, give the bird a few extra treats. On special occasions like Christmas or thanksgiving, include a few gifts for your macaw as well. And, it is so simple to please them. All they need is a new perch or a new toy and they are good to go! This makes them feel like they are a part of some important flock ritual and will make their little hearts swell with joy.

- While you are away doing your chores or when you are out to pick up groceries, you could leave the radio or TV on for your bird. This additionally helps them pick up new words and sentences. Since Scarlet Macaws are good speakers, they will pick up several words. The best shows for birds are cartoon shows as they are loud, cheerful, colorful and have loads of action. Giving your bird a foraging toy is the best thing to do while you are away.

Of course, you need to spend a lot of time with your bird too. Talk to him and make him feel like a part of your family. Once he is acquainted with the family, you can even keep him in the living room while you all enjoy a good movie.

Scarlet Macaws love to cuddle and will do just about anything for those few extra minutes on your lap or shoulder.

## 5. Grooming a Scarlet Macaw

Grooming a Scarlet Macaw is not at all a lot of work. In fact you need to spend a few minutes misting the bird occasionally. This is because birds like the Scarlet Macaw groom themselves regularly. These birds do not like to stay messy and will make sure that their feathers are always clean and in place.

However, grooming is an important bonding activity. In the wild, these birds will preen their mates and keep the other's feathers well in place. If you do the same for your bird, he is likely to form a strong bond with you.

### a. How Scarlet Macaws groom themselves

The process by which birds keep their feathers in good shape and well groomed is called preening. With almost 25000 feathers, it is natural for a bird to want to constantly work towards each one of them to keep them in the best condition. This is a behavior pattern that you will observe with just about any species of birds.

There is a gland called the uropygial gland that is found just below the tail of most birds. This gland releases oils that contain natural waxes that help in keeping the feathers waterproof. In addition to that, the feathers also become more flexible with the application of this oil. Each feather is protected and coated as the bird applies the secretions of this gland on each feather.

What is interesting with Scarlet Macaws and all parrots is that this gland is absent. Instead, the feathers are broken down into fine power that is applied on the body.

There are several advantages of preening besides making the bird look good. Some of the important benefits of preening include:

- Aligning the feathers in such a way that they keep the bird insulated and protected from water.
- The shape of the feathers is maintained in an aerodynamically feasible manner to improve flight.

- Parasites and lice that carry diseases are removed to keep not just themselves but the entire flock safe.

- When the feathers molt, the bird needs to remove a tough coating that is seen on the new feathers. That way the new feathers can be kept in place.

- The bird looks healthier when preened properly and is more likely to attract a mate.

With the bird taking so many measures to groom itself, what could you possibly do to for him? Bathing, feather clipping and toenail clipping are the most important grooming rituals between pet owners and their Scarlet Macaws.

### b. Bathing your Scarlet Macaw

Bathing a Scarlet Macaw is very simple. All you need to do is mist the body of the bird with a spray bottle of water. Only when you see matted feathers should you gently brush the area to remove the debris. Soap is not required to bathe your Scarlet Macaw unless there is a lot of debris that is stuck on the feathers of the bird.

If you do use soap, make sure that it is very mild and that it is thoroughly rinsed off the bird's body. You can even hold the bird under a warm shower. They will enjoy this as it resembles the rain that they are so used to thanks to the rainforests that they originate from.

If the bird turns away from the spray of water and looks uncomfortable, take him out of there immediately. A bird who is enjoying the bath will lift his feathers and turn around to soak the whole body.

Water baths are popular with all breeds of birds. Place a shallow bowl with water and slowly lower the bird into the bath. If your bird is still not hand trained, you can even put a few celery pieces in the water. As the bird forages, he will also bathe himself.

There is a certain season called the molting season when the birds shed old feathers and grow new ones. This is a very uncomfortable phase for the bird as his skin will be highly irritable. To fix this, you can give the bird a good misting with a spray bottle. You can use water that is at room temperature to ease the discomfort.

### c. Wing and toenail clipping

Many people advocate against wing clipping. However, in many cases owners find it easier to manage the bird when he is not able to fly off. Scarlet Macaws are not stopped by cages and if the quality of the cage is not good enough, you may expect several escapes. Even when you are traveling with the bird, keeping the wings clipped is a good idea.

To clip the wings, it is best that you consult a professional if you have not done it before. It will not cost more than $10 or £5 pounds.

If you want to do this at home, it is best to wrap a towel around the bird's body. Then, let one wing come out of the loose end. Cut about 1 cm from the largest feathers that are called the primary feathers. Repeat this on the opposite side and make sure that you cut the feathers equally.

In case you catch a blood feather, you can stop the bleeding with flour. This will not render the bird incapable of flying but will make him get less lift. The wings are used to balance the body as well so cutting feathers on both sides equally is a must.

To clip the toenails, just place your finger below the overgrown part of the nail and file the nail slightly. Do not make it too short as it impairs the bird's ability to climb and hold their food. The nail should only be blunt enough to make sure it does not get stuck to the upholstery around your home.

# Chapter 5: Bonding with your Scarlet Macaw

Bonding time with your Scarlet Macaw is of utmost importance. This is when you try and get the bird to become a part of your household and help him work around troublesome behavior patterns like aggression and biting. Basically, a lot of your bonding time will include training your Scarlet Macaw. But, before you do that, you need to be sure that your bird is in the mood for it. How do you find that out? By observing the body language of the bird.

## 1. Macaw body language

Now vocalization is one thing but birds rely heavily on their body postures to communicate the way they are feeling. You can easily tell whether your bird is happy, angry, bored, tired or unwell just by looking at the posture. Here are a few body language tips that every Scarlet Macaw owner must know about:

The body:

•      If your bird is on your shoulder and is constantly tugging on the collar of your shirt, it means that he wants to get off.

•      If the head of the bird is lowered while the wings are lifted slightly, he wants you to pick him up.

•      If the bird is hanging with one or both feet from the cage, he is in a playful mood.

•      If his rear end rubs the table while he walks back, he is going to take a poop.


The eyes:

•      All parrots exhibit pinning which is rapid dilation of the pupils. This is either done when the bird is excited or when the bird is afraid. You can study the situation to tell how your bird is feeling.

The voice:

•     If the bird is talking, whistling or singing, it means that he is happy and quite content.

•     If he is mumbling to himself or is just chattering softly, he is practicing the words that he learnt.

•     Loud chatter is considered attention seeking behavior.

•     Clicking of the tongue means that the bird is just entertaining himself or is calling you to play with him.

•     Growling is a sign of aggression. There could be something in the room that is bothering him. Removing that object will make him stop immediately.

The beak:

•     If you notice your bird grinding his beak just before he sleeps, it means that he is very happy to be in your home.

•     Clicking of the beak when you pass by is your bird's way of greeting you. At the same time, clicking when you are holding him means that he does not want to be handled by you at the moment.

•     If the beak is on the ground and the feathers are fluffed, he wants you to pet him.

•     If your macaw regurgitates, it is a sign of great affection. They do this only for their mates in the wild.

•     Bobbing the head is a type of attention seeking behavior.

•     If the bird is just rubbing his beak on the perch, he is cleaning himself.

Feet and legs:

•     If your bird is standing upright with his weight equally on both feet, he is content and happy.

•     If the posture of the bird is upright and he is looking at you, it means that he wants you to pick him up right that instant.

- If the bird is feeling restless and impatient, he will rock back and forth on the perch.

- If the bird is standing on one foot, he is relaxed.

- If he is standing on foot with all his feathers fluffed, he is happy.

- If your bird is standing on one foot and has the beak tucked beneath the wing, he is just cleaning himself.

- If he is standing on one foot but is grinding his beak, he is tired.

- If he is standing on one foot with glazed eyes and semi-fluffed feathers, it means that he is falling asleep.

- If the bird is scratching the bottom of the cage, he wants you to let him out.

- Tapping of the feet indicates that the bird is trying to protect his or her territory.

The feathers:

- Ruffled feathers can mean one of the following things:

- The bird is feeling too cold and is trying to warm himself up.

- The bird is trying to relieve tension and stress.

- The bird is sick.

Position of the crest:

- If the crest is lifted, the bird is excited.

- If the crest is puffed up it is seen as a sign or aggression.

- If the crest is flat on the ground while the bird is hissing, it means that he is scared or just getting ready to attack someone.

The tail:

- If the tail is shaking, the bird is preparing for some fun times ahead.

- Tail bobbing means that the bird is tired or is catching his breath after strenuous physical activity. If this behavior is seen even when the bird has not done anything physically demanding, you need to take him to a vet immediately.

•        Fanning of the tail is usually a sign of aggression. The bird is displaying his strength through this body language.

Wings:

•        Flapping of the wings is an attention seeking behavior.

•        Flipping of the wings could indicate one or more of the following:

-        Pain or discomfort

-        Anger and aggression

-        A call for your attention.

•        If the wings of your bird are drooping it is generally a sign that the bird is unwell.

The head:

•        If the head is turned back and tucked below the wing, your bird is asleep.

•        When the head is lowered and turned, your bird finds something very interesting.

•        If the head is down and the wings are extended, your bird is just stretching or yawning.

These simple behavior patterns will help you choose the best time to form that bond with your beloved macaw. Responding aptly to this body language also helps the bird trust you more because you are one of his own now.

## 2. Training your Scarlet Macaw

A well trained bird is always a lot easier to handle and manage. If your Scarlet Macaw has any behavioral issues, they can be sorted with training gradually. But, you need to understand that this takes a lot of patience and can be quite demanding in terms of the time you spend. Here are a few tips that you should keep in mind before you start training your Scarlet Macaw:

- Establish a routine. Practice your training session at a particular time every day.

- Be patient. Do not show your bird that you are irritated or annoyed with him for not pulling off a trick. This is not natural for him and he is bound to take some time.

- Be consistent. Do not change the cues that you give the bird. If you are saying "Up" sometimes and "Come" the other time, the bird may not take the cue.

- Be abundant in your praises. Let your bird know how much you appreciate his efforts.

These tips are very important when you are training any animal. With highly intelligent creatures like Scarlet Macaws, it is a lot more challenging but is great fun too.

## a. Target Training

Target training gives your bird something to look forward to while performing the tasks that you want him to. Target training is the best way to get your bird to do the most basic thing- getting in and out of the cage.

Give your Scarlet Macaw a target that he can follow. This is most likely a treat at the end of a stick. Hold it out to the bird and allow him to take the treat. If your bird does not respond to the target initially, you can gently touch his beak with it and see how he reacts. If it is treat that your bird likes, he will go for it immediately.

Then, gradually increase the distance between your bird and the target and watch him walk up to it and take a nibble. You can then move the target around the cage and see if he follows it.

The next step is to get the bird to follow this target even when the treat is absent. He may do this the first time you present the target without the treat. If the bird does not respond to the target without the treat, then you will have to continue with the treat for a while until he forms the association between the target and the chance of getting a treat with a target.

When your bird is following the target successfully, the next step is to get him in and out of the cage. Open the cage door and hold the target at the door. He will come to take a nibble. Keep pulling it away till the bird is finally out of the cage.

Let the bird explore the area. Make sure it is free from any danger for the bird. If your macaw has the slightest negative experience with the first time in open space, he will take a long time to regain trust.

Then, when you are ready to take the bird back into the cage, allow him to follow the target. Finish off with a treat or a toy in the cage so that he associates the cage with only positive experiences.

## b. Step up training

Stepping up is one of the most important things you will teach your macaw. The Scarlet Macaw is a rather large bird. So, having him step up on a finger can be a little hard. The bird will step up but you may find him too heavy to handle.

The best option is to offer your forearm as the step for a bird like the Scarlet Macaw. So, hold the forearm horizontally in front of the bird and place the target just behind your forearm. Then say the cue word, "Up". The bird will go for the target and will step on your forearm to reach out to it.

If the bird does not step up with the target, you can even hold his favorite treat in the similar fashion. Now, you need you keep your hand very still. The bird may nibble at your forearm. However, you must not flinch or move. An unsteady perch is one thing that all birds dislike. He is biting to make sure that this perch will not break. Chew on your lower lip and hold still.

If the bird steps up, praise him and give him a treat. Repeat this a couple of times and then try to just place your forearm before the bird and say "Up". If he climbs up without the target, you have successfully completed your step up training.

Remember that the bird has an additional incentive for stepping up- being with you. They are most likely going to learn this trick faster than any other trick because of this.

Step up training can then be extended to your shoulder or your head. That way your bird can be with you at all times as soon as you are home from work.

Step up training is also valuable in keeping your bird safe. If you are having an introduction session between your bird and other household pets, there could be some signs of aggression. If you notice this, you can get the bird to step up on your hand and take him out of a potentially dangerous situation. Even when you are escaping a natural calamity or say a fire, you can save your bird easily if he can step up faster.

### c. Managing aggressive behavior

Aggression in Scarlet Macaws is usually an attempt to seek your attention. An aggressive bird will mostly display this aggression by biting. Now, what the bird really wants is your attention. If you scream or shout back at the bird, he will read it as a response. Although it is hard to not scream after a bite from the powerful mandibles of the Scarlet Macaw, it is necessary to keep your calm.

If the bird is perched on your body while displaying the aggressive behavior, you can do two things. First, put the bird back in the cage and ignore him till he calms down. Go to him only when he is relaxed and does not attack upon handling.

The next thing to do would be to run while the bird is perched on you. They will feel unsteady and they really dislike this feeling. If you do this every time your bird bites or nibbles at you, he will make an association with the unpleasant feeling and will eventually stop.

If aggressive behavior is a sudden manifestation, then you need to consult your vet. There are chances that the bird is in heat or has some health issue that is making him or her behave in this manner. Also, spending time with your bird and giving him a lot of attention will reduce aggressive behavior.

### d. Managing screaming

It is a natural thing for your Scarlet Macaw to scream for a few minutes at dawn or dusk. This is their natural way of calling out the flock. While this behavior is acceptable, screaming becomes an issue when it is persistent.

If you notice that your bird is screaming every time you leave him alone, he is only doing this for your attention. The more attention you give him when he screams, the more he is likely to continue the behavior.

When your bird screams, leave the room without any response. If you shout back, he will believe that you are having a conversation with him. This will make him scream even louder.

Come back to your bird only when he is calm. That will help him understand that you will only go to him when he is well behaved. Keeping your parrot mentally stimulated will curb this issue to a large extent.

Whenever you leave the bird alone, give him a foraging toy or even a puzzle toy. That will make him independent and less anxious when he is all by himself.

### e. Teaching your bird to talk

Scarlet Macaws are known to be decent talkers. However, in comparison to other species of parrots like the Eclectus parrot, your Scarlet Macaw is likely to talk a lot lesser.

Birds merely mimic what we say. So repeating words and phrases before the bird is the best way to train them to talk. If you say hello every time you see the bird or "food time" every time you feed him, he will pick up on it and will say the word before you do some day. When he does, give him loads of treats and praise him abundantly.

Speaking to the bird every day and saying the words that you want him to learn in a high and excited voice will make him pick up on it. Another great idea to get your bird to learn words is to play the radio and also cartoons to him. He will pick up on words that he hears often.

You will also notice your bird mumbling these words to himself before he actually says them out loud. This is his way of practicing what he has learnt. It seems like your bird is actually chattering to himself when he is learning words.

### f. Socializing

For a bird as large as the Scarlet Macaw, the owners need to take immense responsibility for the behavior of the bird. Even a friendly nip or bite can lead to severe injuries and problems. And, if your bird causes damages to any third party, you as the owner can even face legal charges.

The first thing that you need to do is to train the macaw for basics like stepping up and even getting in and out of the cage. This is when your macaw is safe to introduce to your guests outside of a cage. Until you are sure that your macaw is through with this training, introducing them to strangers is not the best option.

Actually, as far as your macaw is concerned, guests are invaders in their territory. In addition to this when your guest is excited to see the gorgeous Scarlet Macaw and approaches the bird, it makes him feel helpless. There is another thing that a guest does- he takes the owner's attention away.

In short, having a guest is a negative experience for your bird. You need to make sure that you make it a fun thing for your macaw through positive reinforcements.

So, make sure that your Scarlet Macaw is well socialized, especially when it comes to meeting new people. Because these birds are so easy to train, you can follow these 12 simple steps to make them friendly and also more approachable when you have guests at home.

•       Instruct your guest to ignore the bird: If it is the first time someone is meeting your macaw, ask them to avoid even eye contact for the first 30-60 minutes. If your guest just goes for the cage, the bird will think that he means harm. However, let the guest stay in a room that the bird is able to watch over. That will let him understand that this person does not mean any harm and is actually welcome in the flock.

•       Let the bird out: This should be done only if your bird is used to being handled. Let him out of the cage and let him be. The guest should be instructed not to approach the bird. Let the macaw take his time. These birds are extremely cautious which means that sooner or later, they will either walk over to the guest or will come to you to seek some security. This way, the bird does not get any reason to be scared and is more trusting towards new people.

•       Teach the guest to handle the bird: Once the bird is comfortable to just hang around the new person, you can get them to handle it. Not everyone knows how to handle a pet bird so you have to assist them. Even in case of people who have had pet birds at home, you need to tell them how your bird likes to be handled. Macaws are different from pets like dogs and do not like to be heavily petted. It may turn them against the person as they like to be treated with a lot of dignity.

•       Let them pretend to be a perch: The guest should consider himself a perch that the bird will sit on. So just extending the arm out and finger out and staying still is the best option. They will not reach out for the bird. Instead, you will let the bird go on to their arm or finger. Ask them not to move. Birds like macaws hate an unsteady perch. If your visitor is scared, do not force the bird upon them. If the person is scared, the bird will be scared and will certainly react.

•       Let the person cue tricks: If your macaw has been trained to perform tricks, then it is a wonderful ice breaker. When the bird is comfortable enough, let your guest cue the trick. Then, providing a treat for performing a trick gives the bird some reassurance. This is the safest and most fun way to get your bird to meet new people. It is a positive reinforcement plan that is sure to get your bird more interested in new people.

• Call the bird to step up: This can happen in the second meeting preferable or whenever the bird is fully comfortable with a person. Now, you will step out of the way and will not hand over the bird to the person. Instead, the guest will cue the step up command. Using a target or a treat the first time is a good idea. It is best to do this after the bird has been cued for other tricks. That makes him understand that the new person will give him treats if he does what he is asked to do. There is no room for doubt when the bird has already interacted to some extent.

• Petting: It is good to get your bird accustomed to being petted. But, this should be reserved for when the bird is entirely confident about a certain person. You must guide the person and tell them exactly how your bird likes to be petted. For instance, they may love being scratched on the cheek and may hate being touched on the wing. If the person does the latter, be sure that your macaw will never let him or her touch him again. Start by petting the bird yourself first and let the guest join in. Then you can take your hand away and let the guest take over. This comfortable transition will make your bird look forward to new people being around.

• Pass the bird around: After your macaw is accustomed to a group of people, you can simply pass the bird around from one person to another at intervals. You can even add a resting perch in between where the bird can relax while you entertain your guests. The basic idea is to make sure that your bird is used to many hands. This makes them trust people more and will also make them comfortable in front of a large crowd.

• Make grabbing a positive thing: Grabbing basically means holding the bird from the sides of the body. This training is essential as it helps the bird stay relaxed when he is at the vet, when he is travelling by flights or even when he needs to be grabbed and taken out of an emergency. This is at a much later stage only with people whom the bird knows really well and trusts. They will begin by approaching the bird with a treat, holding on to him and then giving him a treat. This tells your bird that hands are not something that he needs to fear.

Your guest can begin by just touching the bird and giving him a treat, cupping the body and then giving him a treat and then proceeding to actually grabbing him. You will get them to repeat each step as many times as needed to make sure that your bird is completely comfortable before you actually get them to progress into getting their hands closer to

66

the bird. Then, being handled becomes a regular activity for your bird and he will not feel scared.

• Take the bird out on outings: Plan outdoor activities that involve your bird and a few other friends. It can begin with a family dinner or even a casual visit to a friend's place. This prevents the bird from being excessively territorial as he is on neutral grounds. That will make him less nippy and defensive and the interaction is more peaceful. Don't overwhelm the bird by taking him to party or even a gathering with more than ten people.

• Take the bird out: Keeping the bird in the cage and going out for a stroll in the park has also helped many macaw owners claim that this helps the bird make observations and even be calmer in front of strangers as they are accustomed to new faces. There may be people who will ask you if they can handle your bird. If you think that your bird is not aggressive, then you can instruct them to handle the bird safely. Only if they follow your instructions completely will you let them handle your bird.

• Uncontrolled interactions: Once your parrot is comfortable around people, let the interactions be less controlled. If there is a way you would recommend your bird be handled, let the person do just that. If the bird is harmless, he will only freak out momentarily and will get over it very soon. This makes them more robust and will not require you to intervene and protect him at all times.

No matter what you do, never predict how your bird is going to react in any situation. The last thing you want to take for granted is the temperament of your macaw. Remember that these birds are extremely intelligent and sensitive and will analyze each situation they are put in. Be around for all initial interactions and when you are certain that your bird is comfortable, let go slowly.

## 3. Dividing time between your bird and your child

Scarlet Macaws are very gentle and pleasant creatures and are likely to get along with your child if your child is well behaved. If the child teases the bird or hurts him, a negative response is inevitable.

Another reason why children and birds do not get along in some cases is the possessive nature of these birds. They do not like to share the love of their human. In the wild, too, birds that have bonded with one another are going to give each other more preference than the hatchlings too. Scarlet Macaws, especially, are infamous for abandoning their clutch and hatchlings in order to be with their partner.

Of course, you cannot neglect or ignore your child. If you have a newborn, it is always better to wait for some time before you commit to a pet. This is because babies take up a lot of our time and birds like the Scarlet Macaw are quite demanding when it comes to attention and your time.

In some rare cases, it is seen that Scarlet Macaws become overtly noisy and aggressive in the presence of the child. This is because the child is taking up all your time and the bird gets jealous or feels neglected.

Another common habit is going to the bird only after your child has fallen asleep. So, naturally, the bird begins to believe that you are available for him only when the child is not present. This way, your child becomes a negative entity for you parrot.

Balancing your time between the macaw and your child is the most crucial thing to do. One way to do this would be to put your Scarlet Macaw in a temporary travel cage whenever you are feeding the baby or changing him, keep this cage in the room. That will make your bird feel like he is a part of the experience too. Keep talking to your bird, give him a few toys and when he is behaving well, praise him and give him a treat.

When you feel like your bird is ready, you can even let him out of the cage around the child. Watch the response of your child towards the macaw. If the child gets scared and screams or cries, your macaw will also feel threatened. Watch your child for any signs of negative response. The slightest sign should be your cue to remove the macaw from that situation.

You must introduce your Scarlet Macaw to your baby only after he is at least trained to step up. If not, you are putting your child and the bird at risk. Include your child in the feeding and playing sessions with the bird so that he can form positive associations with the little person. This will help the bird form a bond with your child as well. And, for all you know, your Scarlet Macaw may pick your little one as his human!

# Chapter 6: Travelling with your Scarlet Macaw

Travelling is stressful when an exotic bird like the Scarlet Macaw is also part of it. You need to take several measures to ensure that your bird is safe and is more importantly legal to take to a different state or country.

The mode of transport that you choose is very crucial for the health and well-being of your bird. Each one comes with a set of challenges that you need to take care of before you take your bird with you.

## 1. Legal considerations

Almost all species of exotic birds including Scarlet Macaws are protected by strict rules laid out by CITES. If you are planning to travel with your Scarlet Macaw, you need to be sure that you are aware of all these legalities.

First, when you decide to take your bird to another country or state, you will have to check for a permit requirement. Some states will require a permit under the regulations of CITES while others will require you to take a local permit as well. For example, in the United States, you need a CITES permit as well as a permit from the Endangered Species Act. Check for regulations of the wildlife department in your state, country and the country you are travelling to be safe.

The Scarlet Macaw is listed on the Appendix I of CITES. This means that your bird can be taken to another country only under certain circumstances. You will most likely need a permit form the country you are travelling and from the country you are travelling to.

Your veterinarian is a reliable source of information. He will be able to help you obtain these permits as well. You can check the official CITES website and the websites of the Wildlife departments of the countries involved.

Plan your travels well in advance because most permits take two months at least for processing. If you have to make a business trip urgently, you will most probably have to make alternate arrangements for your Macaw.

Here are a few things you need to have when you are planning a trip with your bird:

- Proof that your bird was legally obtained. A breeder's health certificate is usually accepted.

- The permit from the respective countries that you are going to travel to and from.

- Completed declaration forms as required in the destination port.

- A health certificate from your vet that is not more than 30 days old.

Take a few copies of your permits just to be sure. You also need to be prepared to be questioned by authorities at both ports to confirm the reason for import or export of the bird. With all the documents in place, you will not have to worry about your bird too much. Just make sure that his wings are clipped to ease the process of customs.

## 2. Travelling by car

Most birds are used to travelling by cars because they do it so frequently. Some of them simply love this little trip with the family. However, if this is the first time you are going to be taking your Scarlet Macaw with you in the car, there are a few things that you must take care of.

First, get the bird accustomed to the ambience of your car. Transfer him to a travel cage and place the cage in the car for a few minutes. You can leave the windows down or can turn the air conditioner on at room temperature. Never leave the bird in a hot car. In many states, this is considered illegal and is viewed as cruelty against the bird.

The next thing to do would be to get the bird used to the movement. Drive around the block and watch the bird's body language.

If he is singing and perched in an erect posture, he is quite unfazed by the movement of the car. He could even get on to the floor if the perch is shaky. But, the body language will be positive.

On the other hand, if your bird is trembling and has retreated to one corner of the cage, take him back home and put him in the his cage with lots of food and water. Try again after a few days.

As the bird get more comfortable, you can increase the distance of your drive. When you are ready to actually travel with your bird, there are a few preparations that you need to make.

Ensure that there is a lot of clean drinking water available for your bird. You must also have fresh pellets in a bowl for him to eat on the way. The substrate should be thick and have multiple layers. You bird is likely to poop more when he is travelling.

Make sure that you stop the car every half an hour to give the bird a break. He will be able to stop, drink some water and refresh himself. On the way, keep the air-conditioner on at room temperature and keep the cage away from any drafts. Do not keep the window open as it freaks the bird out. Lastly, place the cage in the shade. Or you could put a towel over half the cage as a retreat spot for your bird. The cage should be kept in a way that prevents too much movement.

Avoid loud music. Instead, talk and sing to your bird to make him feel comfortable. When the bird has completed a few trips with you, you won't have to worry about travelling by car as much.

### 3. Travelling by air

Air travel is very stressful for the birds. This is because they are separated from you and are left in a space that is so unfamiliar to them for the entire travel period.

The first thing you need to do is prepare a file with all the necessary travel documents. You will need to keep this handy as they will ask for it on several occasions during your travel.

Book an airline that has good pet travel policies. Some of them will have services like feeding and changing the water for the pets. This is very important to make sure your bird does not get dehydrated during this period.

Next, you will have to book all the transit flights in the same airlines, if any. That way any service or requirement will simply be continued during your travel. With new airlines, you will have to worry about new rules and regulations.

The airlines will give you all the specifications for the travel cage. You will have to get one accordingly. Have several layers of substrate on the floor of the cage. Water should be provided through a bottle-type drinker. Get your bird accustomed to this before he travels or he may not drink any water at all. Only provide pellets to your bird as they are less messy and easy to manage.

A harness for your bird is a good idea. This will help them stay in place in case of any turbulence or disturbance during the flight. You can throw in your bird's favorite toy to make him a little more comfortable.

The bird will have to pass through customs. It is best that you keep his wing clipped so that there are no accidents like a runaway bird in a bust airport.

Even if your bird seems healthy, you need to have him checked the moment you reach home at the destination port. There is a lot of stress when the bird is travelling by air. He could be vulnerable to infections because of this. Of course, you never know how clean the cargo was. So, it is good to have the bird checked as a precautionary measure.

## 4. Making arrangements while you are away

Unless you are moving out permanently, you will probably not have the option of taking your Scarlet Macaw considering the legalities involved.

So, you need to make arrangements for your bird while you are away. Leaving your pet with your friends or relatives is the best option possible. If you have other members in your family, of course, there is no problem at all.

However, in some cases, when you have no one to take care of your bird while you are away, you may have to look for pet sitting services. The Pet Sitters International is an organization that you can depend upon in order to find the best pet sitting services. They have a list of independent pet sitters or pet sitter agencies that you can contact.

It is recommended that you contact local bird clubs to find pet sitters who have worked for the members before and have taken good care of the birds. Friends and family with birds can also provide good recommendations for you.

Now, when you are looking for a pet sitter, you need to conduct an interview with a couple of them till you can find someone reliable enough to leave your bird with. During the interview sessions, there are a few pointers that you need to keep in mind to find the perfect caretaker for your bird.

- Ask for the pet sitters' experience. They should have some knowledge about handling birds and taking care of them. If you see that your pet sitter is a novice, you should know that he at least has birds of his own.

- Ask them what they know about Scarlet Macaws and if they have taken care of these birds in the past. The Scarlet Macaw is a large bird and has very specific requirements. One should know how to handle the bird at least. It is not the same as a Sun Conure or a smaller breed of parrot.

• Ask if they have birds of their own. Anyone who has their own pets will also be sensitive to the requirements of other people. They will be sensitive and will understand that you need the best care for your bird. They are also aware of basic body language and will be able to communicate better with your bird. A pet sitter is not someone who will just feed the birds and clean the cage. They are literally taking your place while you are away.

• Observe the way he or she handles the bird. If they are comfortable with the bird and are able to manage him or her well, then they are probably quite experienced. They must also be able to calm a bird down when he is excited or aggressive.

• You need to make sure that he or she is capable of handling an emergency. Ask them how they would deal with various emergency situations. If it is close to what you would do, then you can hire this individual without a second thought.

• In your absence, if they have a personal emergency, how will they deal with it? Will they be able to send in a substitute? If yes, you need to meet the person who will be substituting for your pet sitter to ensure that they are right for your bird, too.

Once you have finalized upon a sitter, you need to discuss the cost and the services that he or she will provide. Make sure that you have it all in writing to prevent any confusion in the future.

Get all the contact details of your pet sitter including the phone number and email ID. You need to have access to him or her whenever you need. Make it a point to call every day to keep an eye on your bird.

Provide all the contact details of the place that you will be staying in. You also need to provide emergency contact numbers of friends and family members.

Make a written routine for your sitter to follow. You must even include the number of your vet in this list. Ensure that your pet sitter knows where the food is stocked, how to clean the food bowls and the cage and also where the first aid kit is located.

The first time you leave your bird is the hardest. You will eventually get accustomed to one pet sitter who can take care of all your bird's needs. It is best to find a sitter who will stay at your place and take care of the bird. This reduces a lot of stress on the part of your Scarlet Macaw.

Travelling is one of the biggest points for consideration when you bring home a Scarlet Macaw. If you are a frequent traveler, do not bring a bird home.

When you have to take decisions like moving out of a country, think about your Scarlet Macaw. If your bird cannot go with you, are you willing to put him in foster care? If not, then you will have to make compromises on your travel for this.

Only when you are willing to make these sacrifices should you bring a Scarlet Macaw home.

# Chapter 7: Breeding Scarlet Macaws

Scarlet Macaws show maximum behavioral changes among all species of macaws when they reach sexual maturity. They normally become sexually mature at the age of 3 or 4 years. The thing with Scarlet Macaws is that they are monogamous. This means that they mate for life and have the same partner for a lifetime.

In the wild, these pairs are always seen together. Unless one of them is brooding or caring for chicks, they will be in pairs at all times. Showing affection to the partner is quite common with Scarlet Macaws and they usually are seen preening, feeding or licking one another.

Scarlet Macaws nest every one year or every alternate year. This is determined by the weather conditions, the seasonal changes and the availability of food. The breeding season begins in the month of December for birds that are seen in the southern part of their habitat. In case of birds that are see in the northern parts, breeding takes place towards the end of December or in January.

Scarlet Macaws are cavity nesters. This means that they raise their young in the holes of trees that are either dead or really tall. In some cases, they may even occupy the nest that has been left by some other bird. They commonly inhabit the nests of woodpeckers but may, occasionally, make a cavity in the softer snags of trees.

A clutch consists of a maximum of 4 eggs. Usually only two eggs are seen in each clutch. The role of the female is to brood and incubate the eggs while the male protects their nesting area and even brings home food for the young. If needed, the male also helps in brooding.

An egg takes about 28 days of incubation to hatch. As per the age of the hatchlings, they are fed between 4 and 15 times every day. The younger they are, the more they are fed. This is because older birds are able to hold a lot more food in their crop and can be fed more each time.

After about 140 days, the chicks fledge or leave the nest. Then they become fully independent after a year. The interesting thing about Scarlet Macaw parents is that they do not start one more brood unless the previous one is fully secure!

The most common triggers for breeding in Scarlet Macaws include:

- Availability of light: If you want to curb the behavior, you need to reduce the hours of light that are available to the bird. On the other hand, when you want them to reproduce, you can increase light using artificial lighting as well. Light affects the hormonal activity of the bird and helps in promoting or reducing sexual behavior.

- Do not give the bird a suitable nesting area. Make sure that items like cardboard boxes, dark spaces near curtains and even shoes are not available to the bird. When they do not have any nesting space, they are less likely to breed.

- The diet plays an important role in the hormonal activity of the bird. If you reduce the levels of fat, proteins and starch, the bird is less likely to be inclined towards breeding.

- Petting the back or the area near the vent should be avoided, as it is perceived as sexual petting.

If you do decide to find a mate for your bird, you need to first get the bird that you bring home sexed. That is the best way to determine the gender of the bird. With sexually dimporphic birds like the Scarlet Macaw, it is necessary to do this as they look alike and it is very easy for you to get duped.

# 1. Finding your bird a mate

In case you plan to breed a Scarlet Macaw, it is best that you bring home a pair right from the beginning. Your breeder will be able to sell paired birds to you. That reduces the stress of introducing birds and hoping that the bird finds a mate. There are three types of pairs that are generally sold:

- **Proven Pair:** These birds have produced a clutch of eggs at some time of their mating period.

- **Producing Pair:** These birds have recently either laid a clutch or have raised their own young.

- **Bonded pair:** These birds are just compatible and have shown mate behavior towards each other but have not reproduced yet.

The proven and producing pairs are usually more expensive than buying birds of the opposite gender separately. This is because the former are likely to breed faster.

When you are choosing a mate for your Scarlet Macaw, it is best to go back to the same breeder because you have an idea about the quality of raising the birds. If you are going to a new breeder, however, make sure that the bird you get home is healthy.

You can even ask your breeder to help you find a partner for your bird. This may involve your bird spending a few hours at the breeder's aviary to see which bird he is most compatible with. Of course, your breeder will take the necessary quarantining measures to ensure that your birds are nothing short of perfect in health.

The bird that you choose should be tested by a vet. It is a good idea to have a proper physical test, complete blood count and a culture test done in order to determine any potential risks to your bird or to the flock in your home. Of course, the bird should look well physically with all the feathers in shape, the beak smooth and shiny and the legs free from any growth or issues.

When you bring your new bird home, you need to be extremely cautious while introducing them to one another. Make sure you introduce them in a neutral territory to ensure that your pet bird does not get too dominant.

Quarantining is a must with a new bird. A 30 day quarantining process is required. Keep the bird in a separate cage in a separate room for this period. If the bird shows no signs of illness, it is safe to shift the cage of the new bird to your pet's room.

Make sure you monitor the first few interactions to ensure safety of either bird. If they growl, display fanning of the tail feathers or are aloof, put them back in their respective cages and introduce them again.

Only when the birds get used to one another should they be allowed to be in one cage. You will need to keep them in a new cage to avoid any chances of territorial behavior. Observe the birds. You can start off with a few hours in the same cage and gradually increase the time.

When your birds are in heat, the natural progression is for them to mate with one another. They will begin to show very distinct mating behaviors. The male will lower his head and will spread open the wings in an attempt to woo the female. He will also preen her feathers and will feed her. The female reciprocates with the same type of behavior.

This is when you need to begin preparing for the breeding season as mentioned in the section below.

## 2. Preparing for the breeding season

Birds require very specific conditions in order to breed. They are shy creatures and will not breed if there is too much disturbance. You need to first shift the cage of the birds to a room in the house that is quiet, but has a good supply of natural light. You can lay a cloth over the cage for the birds to escape into when they want to rest.

Unless there is a proper nesting place available for the birds, they are very unlikely to mate. Keeping a nesting box just outside the cage will encourage them to mate. It can be placed on the play area of you have a play top cage.

Instead of using cardboard boxes, it best to get a store bought nesting box for your Scarlet Macaw. These nesting boxes made of wood or metal are not destroyed easily. They can be used for all the breeding seasons making the birds feel comfortable. These boxes are also easier to clean. You need to remember that Scarlet Macaw chicks can be very messy.

Choose a vertical nesting box that measures at least 18X18X36 inches. These boxes usually have an entrance door and a separate inspection door that you can access.

The nesting box should be placed in such a way that the birds have a good view of the room around them. The cage should have solid perch for the birds. Place one inside the cage and one outside leading to the next box. This allows them to access the nest. These perches should be made of hardwood as the females are likely to chew on them when they become hormonal.

Leaving a few soft wood options is a good idea to help the bird chew it and release some stress. With this arrangement, your birds will get ready to mate. The male will mount the female a couple of times. In two weeks the female will lay her first clutch of eggs that consists of 2-4 eggs that are white in color.

The incubation period is about 22 days during which the hen will care for the eggs on her own.

### Diet for the breeding season

You need to make sure that the birds have adequate nutrients to produce the necessary hormones and have a successful breeding season. For the females, especially, the diet is of utmost importance.

Adding assorted nuts to the diet will help the bird to a large extent. Each nut has specific functions that aid the breeding season. Here are a few nuts that you should include and the benefits of these nuts:

- Macadamia nuts- They provide the additional fats that are required in a bird's diet during this season.
- Walnuts- They provide the birds with necessary omega 3 fatty acids.
- Filberts- They are a great source of calcium for the females.
- Pistachios- They aid vitamin A in large amounts.

In addition to that you can also provide coconut, eggs and fresh fruits and vegetables. The nutrition of the bird determines the final quality of the eggs that are produced during this season.

You can even provide fortified pellets or supplements under the guidance of your vet to give your birds the additional nutrition boost that they require.

## 3. Artificial incubation of the eggs

Scarlet Macaws are known to be terrible parents. They usually abandon their clutch after a few days. This is when you need to intervene and take care of the eggs yourself. Sometimes you will also notice that the hen also destroys a couple of the eggs.

To incubate the eggs, you can purchase a standard incubator from any pet supplies store. You can also order the online. It is never advisable to prepare your own incubator as the temperature settings need to be very accurate to hatch the eggs successfully. The incubation period will be the same as the natural incubation period.

The incubator is a one-time investment that is completely worth it if you choose to breed more Scarlet Macaws even in the next season.

Here are a few tips to incubate the eggs correctly:

- Pick the eggs up with clean hands. The chicks are extremely vulnerable to diseases and can be affected even with the smallest traces of microbes. Only pick eggs that are visibly clean. If there is a lot of debris or poop on a certain egg, it is best not to mix it with the other eggs as it will cause unwanted infections.

- Wash the eggs gently to clean the surface. The next step is to candle the eggs. This means you will have to hold the egg up to a light. If you can see the embryo in the form of a dark patch, it means that the egg is fertile. On the other hand, if all you can see is an empty space inside the egg, it is probably not going to hatch.

- In the natural setting, the eggs are usually given heat on one side while the other side remains cooler. Then the hen may turn the eggs with her movements. It is impossible to heat the egg evenly even if you have a fan type incubator that heats up the interior of the egg quite evenly.

- The next thing to keep in mind is the transfer from the nest box to the incubator. Line a container with wood shavings and place the eggs away from each other. Even the slightest bump can crack an egg. You need to know that a cracked egg has very few chances of hatching.

- The incubator will also have a humidifier that will maintain the moisture levels inside the incubator. The temperature and the humidity should be set as per the readings advised for macaws. That is the ideal condition for the eggs to hatch.

- In case you want to be doubly sure, you can also check the temperature with a mercury thermometer regularly.

- It is safest to place the eggs on the side when you put them in the incubator. They are stable and will not have any damage or accident.

- Heating the eggs evenly is the most important thing when it comes to the chances of hatching the egg. Make sure you turn the eggs every two hours over 16 hours. This should be done an odd number of times. The next step is to turn the eggs by 180 degrees once every day.

- Keep a close watch on the eggs in the incubator. It is best that you get an incubator with a see-through lid. This will let you observe and monitor the eggs. If you notice that one of them has cracked way before the incubation period ends, take it out of the incubator. If the eggs have a foul smelling discharge, begin to take an abnormal shape or change color, you need to remove them as they could be carrying diseases that will destroy the whole clutch.

- Usually, Scarlet Macaw eggs will pip after 24-48 hours of the completion of the incubation period.

- The hatching of the egg begins when the carbon dioxide levels in the egg increase. This starts the hatching process. All baby birds have an egg tooth which allows them to tear the inner membrane open. Then they continue to tear the egg shell to come out.

- The muscles of the chick twitch in order to strengthen them and to make sure that he is able to tear the egg shell out successfully.

- Never try to assist the hatching process unless you are a professional. If you feel like your chicks are unable to break out of the egg shell, you can call your vet immediately.

Watching the eggs hatch is a magical experience. You can do a few small things to make your clutch more successful. For instance, if you are buying a brand new incubator, turn on the recommended settings and keep it on for at least two weeks before you expect the eggs to be placed in them.

Make sure that the incubator is not disturbed. Keep all the wires tucked in to prevent someone from tripping on it and disturbing the set up or turning the incubator off. It is best to place this incubator in areas like the basement that are seldom used by you or your family members.

## 4. Raising the chicks

Towards the end of the incubation period, you need to set up a brooding box which can either be purchased or even created using a simple card board box. This is where the chicks will be raised until they are large enough to feed on their own and occupy a cage.

Now, this box needs to have an internal temperature of 36 degrees centigrade. You can maintain this using a heating lamp. If you do not feel confident to do this, you can just buy a readymade brooder. These brooders have recommended settings that will ensure that your bird is in safe hands.

As soon as the egg hatches, the hatchlings should be shifted to this brooder or brooding box.

Young birds are seldom able to feed on their own. You will have to make sure that you give the birds the nutrition that they need by hand-feeding them.

Your vet will be able to recommend a good baby bird formula that you can feed the hatchlings. All you have to do is mix the formula as per the instructions on the box. Then using a clean syringe or ink dropper, you can feed the babies.

When you are feeding the bird, make sure that you place him on a towel because this is going to be a rather messy task. Then hold the head of the bird between two fingers and push the upper jaw gently. The bird will open his mouth automatically. Then, you will have to hold the syringe to the left of the bird's mouth or to your right and then let the food in. This ensures that your bird does not choke on the food that you are giving him.

When the birds are done eating, they will automatically refuse the feed. You will have to feed hatchlings at least once every two hours. Make sure that you watch the body language of the bird. If he is resisting the feed, you can wait a little longer and then do the same.

As the birds grow, the number of feeding sessions will reduce. Ideally, by the time the feathers of the birds appear, they will be feeding about three times every day.

The next step is to wean the birds or make them independent eaters. This can be done when the birds are about 7 weeks old. You can introduce solid foods like pellets and fruits to the bird along with the handfed formula.

Just place a few pieces of fruit or some pellets in front of the bird and wait for him to taste it. If he likes it, he may eat a little and then move on to the formula. Try introducing different fruits and vegetables and notice which ones are tempting enough for the bird to leave the formula for.

You can replace one meal with the favorite food of the bird and add a few pellets too. You will notice that eventually the birds will eat when they are hungry and will not accept the hand fed formula. That is when they are fully weaned.

Incubating the egg artificially has several advantages. To begin with, it encourages the parent birds to lay another clutch of eggs. Next, it increases the chances of the egg hatching. As for hand feeding, it makes your birds familiar with people and will also make them easier to train. Scarlet

Macaws are known to be bad at parenting and are notorious for leaving their babies hungry.

On the other hand, when a bird is raised by the parents, they will develop a parenting instinct that is better than that of a hand fed bird. They are likely to be better breeders.

The best thing to do would be to allow the birds to feed the little ones for a while. Then you can intervene and help the babies wean. This is called mixed parenting and is best for those who intend to breed Scarlet Macaws commercially.

# Chapter 8: Scarlet Macaw Health

The most important thing to keep in mind is to constantly monitor the health of your Scarlet Macaw. When you are unable to identify the common illnesses in the initial stages, they manifest into something that can be potentially hazardous to your beloved bird.

Now, with most birds, it is very easy to identify when they are under the weather. They will display some very obvious changes in their behavior that you will be able to notice if you are a hands on bird parent.

## 1. Identifying a Sick Scarlet Macaw

Many parrot owners have spoken about unexpected deaths of their pets. While there are some diseases that have very low incubation periods, most can be detected quite easily at an early stage if the owner is able to recognize the signs of illness in the bird. This is what you need to watch out for:

- Abnormal droppings: The droppings of the bird are the first sign of any illness. The consistency of the poop and its color determine which part of the body has been affected. These are a few abnormalities that you need to keep in mind:
    - Any air pockets in the poop is a sign of gas development in the bird's gut.

    - Dropping which is black or red in color is a sign of egg binding, infection of the intestine or internal bleeding that may be caused by swallowing a foreign object.

    - If any undigested food is excreted, it shows that the bird may have problems in the Pancreas or has an infection of some sort.

    - Diarrhea or loose stools is a sign of multiple issues like infections, parasites or even digestive issues.

    - If your bird has been dropping very liquidy poop for more than two days, it is a sign of some infection in the kidney.

84

-      If the urine content or the transparent liquid part of the poop is low, your bird is possibly dehydrated.

-      If the semi solid part of the dropping is yellow or green in color, it suggests a liver condition.

-      If the urine is yellow in color, it is a chance of a kidney condition.

• There are fluctuations in the weight: You need to have a gram scale in your home and measure your bird from time to time. Of course, there are minute changes based on how much your bird has eaten, the pooping cycle etc. However, if you notice that your bird has lost more than 10% of his total body weight, you need to consult your vet immediately.

• Change in physical appearance: You will notice signs like discoloration of feathers, puffed up feathers and dried poop near the vent. There could be other signs that raise caution. Remember that Scarlet Macaws are fastidious in keeping their body clean. So, a bird who looks messy is possibly unwell.

• Loss of appetite: Scarlet Macaws are good eaters. However, if you notice that they are leaving their food untouched, it is a matter of concern. Even if your bird does not seem fatigued or low in energy, a loss of appetite is a sign of possible illness.

• Withdrawn body language: If your bird retreats to one corner of the cage and spends most of the time on the floor, he is showing signs of illness. In addition to that, the feathers may droop and he may even keep his beak hidden under the wings.

• Discharge of fluids: If you see any discharge from the nasal passage or the eyes, it is a sign of infection. This needs to be attended to immediately.

• Inactivity: Scarlet Macaws are extremely active birds. They love to climb, fly and play. If your bird is less vocal or shows a sudden drop in his levels of physical activity, rush him to a vet immediately.

- Cloudy eyes: A Scarlet Macaw has beady eyes that always sparkle like they are up to some mischief. But, when they are unwell, the eyes become dull and seem quite cloudy.

These are the most common signs of illness in Scarlet Macaws. Of course, they may develop other behavioral problems like biting or fear of people when they are hurt or unwell. Even if it is no illness at all, when you notice the slightest deviation from the norm, take your bird to a vet immediately. As they say, prevention is better than cure, especially in birds that can develop fatal conditions overnight.

## 2. Common Illnesses

For the most part, Scarlet Macaws are hardy birds that are quite immune to most illnesses. However, there are a few infections and diseases that you need to know about as they commonly affect the Scarlet Macaw as a species. We will talk about the identification, the cause and the cure for these conditions in the following section:

### Proventricular Dilation Disease

This condition is also known as Macaw Wasting Syndrome. In the past, this condition was considered to be fatal most of the time. However, new treatment methods have emerged over the years which makes it possible to control the symptoms in the early stages.

This condition is caused by the Avian Bornavirus which is believed to have spread rampantly due to pet trade across the world. These viruses invade the cell of the host and continue to infect more cells eventually. The incubation period for this virus is about 4 weeks. It affects younger birds usually although a Scarlet Macaw is vulnerable at any age, especially during the breeding season. It can be spread from the hen to the eggs as well.

The common signs of PDD are:

- Poor digestion
- Traces of undigested foods in the feces.
- Sudden increase or decrease in appetite
- Weight loss
- Depression
- Anorexia
- Lack of coordination
- Seizures

- Muscle deficiencies
- Feather plucking
- Constant crying or moaning

The treatment of this condition includes administration of anti-inflammatory drugs that can soothe the symptoms. However, the infection itself is seldom cured. Supplements like milk thistle and elemental formula for avians are also recommended.

### Psittacine Beak and Feather Disease

With this condition, the cells of the feather and beak are killed by a strain of virus called the circovirus. This disease also impairs the immune system of the bird, leading to death of the bird from other infections in most cases.

This condition was first noticed among cockatoos but has affected several species of birds, mostly those belonging to the Psittacine family.

In most cases, death follows the infection. However, if the bird responds positively to the tests but has no signs of the diseases physically, it means that he or she is a carrier of the condition. This is when you have to quarantine the bird immediately. This is a contagious disease that spreads very easily.

The common signs of PBFD are:

-        Abnormalities in the feathers
-        Bumps and uneven edges in the beak
-        Missing lumps of feathers
-        Loss of appetite
-        Diarrhea
-        Regurgitation

In most cases, the birds will die before they show the above symptoms.

Treatment of the condition includes administering probiotics and mineral or vitamin supplementation. The only way to curb PBFD is to take preventive measures such as maintaining good sanitation and diet.

### Psittacosis

This condition is also known as Chlamydiosis or Parrot Fever. The threat with this condition is that it can also affect human beings. It is a condition caused by a certain strain of bacteria called the Chlamydia Psittaci.

A few species of birds may never show symptoms of this condition and could be mere carriers. However, the fact that humans are susceptible to the condition requires you to take additional precautions.

This bacterial infection is only spread when you come in contact with the feces of the bird. This is true for other birds as well. So, maintaining good hygiene is the first step towards preventing this condition among the other birds in your aviary. You must also make sure that your birds are not exposed to the feces of wild birds when you let them out. The common problems leading to chlamydiosis are overcrowding of the aviary, improper quarantine measures etc.

The common signs of Chlamydiosis or Psittacosis are:
-       Labored breathing
-       Infection of the sinuses
-       Runny nasal passage
-       Discharge and swelling of the eyes
-       Ruffled feathers
-       Lethargy
-       Dehydration
-       Weight loss
-       Abnormal droppings

These are the mild symptoms of the condition. In case of a chronic case of Psittacosis you will observe unusual positioning of the head, tremors, lack of co-ordination, paralysis of the legs and loss of control over the muscles.

The birds suspected with this condition are tested for a high WBC count and an increase in liver enzymes, which suggests liver damage. Antibiotics like Doxycycline and Tetracycline are usually administered to affected birds. In addition to that supplements and medicated foods are also provided. However, because most birds refuse to eat when affected with this condition, it becomes a lot harder to give them proper treatment.

**Aspergillosis**
This is a condition that is non contagious but highly infectious. The fungus that causes this condition is known as Aspergillus Fumigatus and is known to be very opportunistic. That is why, even the slightest signs of dampness will become breeding grounds for this fungi.

Young birds are mostly susceptible to this condition. In case of juvenile or baby birds, the rate of mortality is extremely high. Of course, in case of adult birds, they could become infected too. The spores of this fungus are easily inhaled as they are extremely small. That is why, the infection is mostly seen in the air capillaries of the affected bird.

The most common signs of aspergillosis include:

- Polydipsia or abnormal thirst
- Stunted growth
- Lethargy
- Ruffled feathers
- Anorexia
- Polyuria or large amounts of urine in the excreta
- Wheezing
- Coughing
- Nasal Discharge
- Tremors
- Ataxia or loss of control over the limbs
- Cloudy eyes

This condition mainly affects the respiratory tract. However, other organs may also be affected in some rare cases of infection. Treatment of this condition is challenging because of the loss of immunity in birds. So the affected bird could also have multiple infections caused by other microorganisms. Normally, systemic antifungal therapy is recommended. The lesions caused at the site of infection may also be removed through suction or surgery.

Preventive care is the best way to keep your bird safe. Maintaining a high standard of husbandry will help you control infections by depriving the fungus of any breeding sites.

**Avian sinusitis**
It is quite common for the sinuses of the birds to get infected. This condition is mostly associated with a deficiency in Vitamin A. This leads to abnormal cell division that will be seen in the form of thickened mucus around the eyes. This can further lead to abscesses or conjunctivitis in the affected bird. There are debates about the causal factor, however.

The earliest signs of this condition are:
- Clicking
- Proptosis or protrusion of the eyeball
- Sneezing

- Excessive secretion of mucus

Later on, you will notice that there is swelling around the eyes as well as the region around the beak of the bird. When the sinus is infected, it is also possible for the bird to be suffering from associated conditions, such as pneumonia.

A needle biopsy of the area with swelling helps diagnose the condition. This helps you differentiate the condition form abscesses that require a completely different treatment altogether.

The bird is treated with an antibiotic called Baytril that can curb any infection by bacteria such as pseudomonas. In addition to this, the bird also requires Vitamin A supplementation which may be administered through an intramuscular injection. The sinus is flushed if the swelling is too much.

You must also improve the diet of the bird and include as many dark green vegetables as possible. Oranges are also recommended to improve the condition. Lastly, you need to include only fortified pellets in your bird's diet to help restore the Vitamin A levels in the body.

## Psittacine Herpes Virus

Also known as Pacheco's disease, this condition was first recognized in the country of Brazil. Aviculturists observed that birds began to die within few days of being unwell. In less than 3-4 days, a herpes virus infection will cause nasal discharge and abnormal feces. This condition is very contagious and is often fatal.

New World parrots like the Scarlet Macaw are more susceptible to this condition. This condition is generally transmitted through the feces or the nasal discharge. The problem with this virus is that it remains stable even outside the body of the host.

It will be seen on different surfaces in the cage, the food and the water bowls. As a result, it spreads quite easily. Of course, there are possibilities of transmission of this condition from the mother to the embryo.

In many cases, a bird could be a mere carrier of the condition without any symptoms. A bird that has survived an infection is a potential threat to you flock.

The symptoms of this condition commonly include:

- Ruffled Feathers
- Diarrhea
- Sinusitis
- Anorexia
- Conjunctivitis
- Tremors in the neck, legs and wings
- Lethargy
- Weight loss
- Green colored Feces

In most cases, death occurs due to enlargement in the liver or the spleen. When subjected to stress and sudden climate changes, the virus can get activated in birds that are carriers, leading to their death.

A PCR test is conducted to screen the birds for a herpes virus infection. In some cases a bird that is tested positive could show no symptoms at all.

There is no known cure for this condition. Only preventive measures can be taken by keeping the cage conditions pristine. You also need to ensure that your bird does not undergo any stress or trauma. When he is not well exercised or mentally stimulated, there are chances of activation of this strain of virus.

**Coacal papillomas**

This is yet another condition that is said to be caused by a strain of virus called Papillomavirus. This condition leads to benign tumors in the regions of the bird's body that are unfeathered. There are a few debates about the causal factors of this condition, however. This is because of the internal lesions detected with this condition that is caused by a strain of Herpes virus.

Common symptoms of the condition include:
- Wart like growths on the legs and feet
- Loose droppings
- Dried fecal matter around the vent area
- Blood in the droppings of the bird

In case you suspect this condition in your macaw, you can make a preemptive diagnosis at home. Apply a small amount of 5% acetic acid on the cloacal region. If this turns white, then your bird is mostly infected.

Proper diagnosis includes a biopsy of the tissue that is affected. The growth on the legs and feet will be removed surgically as the first step to treatment. This condition leads to a compromised immune system that can further lead to secondary infections by bacteria and other microorganisms.

If your bird harbors any internal papillomas, you need to have them monitored frequently for any infection in the GI tract. If left ignored, it can lead to tumors in the bile duct or the pancreas.

**Kidney dysfunction**

There are two kinds of kidney dysfunction that you will observe in birds:

**Chronic renal failure:** This is when the kidney becomes progressively dysfunctional. At the onset, the bird will show very few signs and will only seem mildly under the weather.

**Acute renal failure:** This is when both the kidneys fail and deteriorate rapidly. The condition is usually reversible but the kidneys will be compromised to a great extent.

So, how can you tell if your bird has any developed of these kidney diseases:

- Polydipsia, or excessive water consumption, followed by frequent urination is common. This is the bird's attempt to flush out toxins from the blood as the kidney is unable to perform this function effectively.
- Watery droppings
- Enlargement of the abdomen
- Constipation
- Vomiting
- Inability to fly
- Fluffing of feathers
- Depression
- Lethargy
- Weakness
- Blood in the droppings
- Dehydration
- Swollen joints
- Inability to walk or balance himself

These renal diseases can be caused by microbial infections. The common virus responsible for this condition is the Polyomavirus while the most common fungus seen is the Aspergillus fungi.

There are various other causes like excessive vitamin D consumption, allergy to any antibiotics or medication that has been administered, heavy metal poisoning, toxicity by pesticides and ingestion of certain plants.

Gout, which is the inability of the bird to release waste from the body, also leads to kidney failure over time.

Proper diagnosis of this condition requires a full medical history of the bird. This is followed by a physical examination, blood chemistry tests, blood count tests and a urine analysis. In ambiguous cases, cloacal swabs, endoscopy and ultrasound are used to confirm the condition that the bird has been affected with.

Supportive care, including tube feeding and providing the right supplements, aids recovery of the bird. It is recommended that the blood of the bird be tested on a regular basis to change the treatment method as required by the body of the bird.

Antibiotics may be administered as bacteria is the common cause of renal failure in birds. There could also be some secondary infections that need to be treated with an antibiotics. Besides this, depending upon the nature of the infection, antifungal and antiviral medicines are provided.

In case of toxicity or gout, vitamin A supplementation is encouraged. There could also be surgical intervention if tumors or lesions are detected internally.

It is recommended that you include proteins, vitamin B complex, Vitamin C and Vitamin A in the diet of the bird. Foods like Dandelion root, Cranberry, Parsley and Nettle tea will help improve the functioning of the kidneys and will aid in quick recovery of the affected bird.

**Lipomas or Tumors**

It is possible for pet birds to develop tumors or lipomas on their bodies. These are usually seen as bumps or lumps on the skin or just under the skin. Of course, every lump is not an indication of tumor as some of them could also be abscesses.

In many cases, what is feared to be a tumor could be a cyst that is covered with fluids or pus. These are not cancerous and will not spread like the tumors.

A tumor is a solid tissue mass that can grow very quickly and spread across the body of the bird. It can occur in any part of the body and need immediate attention to ensure that your bird is able to recover from it.

There are two kinds of tumors: Benign and malignant. The benign tumors do not cause cancer while the malignant ones are cancerous. While both can adversely affect the health of the bird, benign tumors are less urgent that the malignant ones.

The reason for this is that the benign tumors do not spread to other parts of the bird's body like the malignant ones. There are chances of growth in this tumor but they almost never spread. Even if they do, there is enough time to provide medical care effectively.

That does not mean that you can ignore these tumors. They need to be removed at the earliest. Since they get bigger in size, they can put a lot of pressure on the internal organs of the bird leading to severe discomfort and even damage.

Malignant tumors will damage the nearby tissues of the affected organ as well. A process called metastasis is responsible for this. This is when the cell breaks away from the tumor and travels through the blood stream. Then it spreads to various parts of the body to cause multiple tumors.

Usually a tumor is caused by mutations in the DNA of the bird's cells. Normal cells will not divide uncontrollably like the tumors. They multiply enough to grow and repair the body.

There are several other factors like the environment of the bird, inclusion of carcinogens in the diet of the bird, nutritional deficiencies, old age and interbreeding that compromises the immune system of the bird, leading to this condition.

There are various types of tumors that can affect a bird. The most common one is that of the skin or the squamous cells of the skin. This leads to tumors near the eyes, around the preen gland, on the skin on the head and around the beak. A huge causal factor for this is self-mutilation by the birds. This is an external tumor that you can identify as lumps on the surface of the skin.

Another type of tumor that affects birds is a fibroid tumor. This affects the connective tissues of the bird. Usually, these tumors are benign. When they become malignant, the condition is known as fibrosarcoma. These tumors are also external and will be seen on the legs, wings, the beak and the sternum of the bird.

The most common type of internal tumor is a tumor in the reproductive organs or the kidneys. Again, these tumors could either be malignant or benign. The problem with these internal tumors is that they will go unnoticed until the bird falls severely sick. The pressure of these tumors on the internal organs leads to a lot of discomfort and stress for the birds. In most cases, the digestive system experiences a lot of stress, leading to improper digestion of food. The droppings are not excreted effectively from the body either. It can also put a lot of pressure on the nervous system, making the bird uncoordinated.

Birds can also develop cancers in the lymphatic system. This compromises the immune system to a large extent leading to secondary bacterial, viral or fungal infections. When the tumor is malignant, the condition is known as lymphoma. It is characterized by swollen lymph nodes in most cases.

Another type of tumor in the birds are lipomas. These are made mostly of mature fat cells. You will find these tumors just under the skin of the bird near the abdomen and the chest. They interfere with the body movements and will also lead to lethargy and inactivity. These are normally seen in obese birds.

Tumors that are external are easily identified as they appear in the form of lumps. Any abnormal growth on the body should be shown to the vet immediately. A pathologist will examine samples from the affected area and will determine if it is a tumor or not. The next step is to check if it is malignant or benign.

The internal tumors are really hard to detect. You will notice symptoms like:
- Loss of weight
- Increased sleep
- Loss of appetite
- Inability to balance the body

- Lameness

These symptoms could be indicative of any other disease as well. So, you need to have your bird checked by a vet the moment you notice them.

Treatment of tumors or lipomas includes surgical removal of the mass of cells. If the tumor is growing or changing and is located in a part of the body that can affect its daily activities, surgery is avoided.

Prognosis of benign tumors is definitely better than the malignant ones. It could just require removal of the tissue in most cases.

It is the malignant tumors that are harder to treat. This is because they may continue to spread even after removal, unless they are removed at a very early stage.

Tumors of the kidney, the liver and other vital organs are the hardest to deal with as they could lead to death of the bird during surgery due to excessive bleeding.

In the case of Scarlet Macaws, it is a lot easier thanks to the size of the birds. The larger the animal, the easier it is to carry out surgical processes.

In rare cases, radiation and chemotherapy may help control these malignant tumors. They will be used in conjunction with surgical processes.

This is a very recent practice in avian medicine. That is why most avian vets will have less experience with providing radiation to birds. However, when there are very few avenues of treatment, radiation may be used on an experimental basis.

The drugs used in chemotherapy are very harsh. Since birds are easily susceptible to toxicity, there are chances that the bird dies of poisoning in the course of this treatment.

If the tumor is malignant, there is very little chance of survival unless the bird is treated in the initial stages. That is why it is recommended to take your bird for regular check-ups by the veterinarian. That way the tests will be able to detect internal tumors, if any.

## Toxicity

Metal poisoning due to metals like zinc and lead is quite common in pet birds. This is because of the several sources of toxicity that we neglect while getting the house bird proofed.

Zinc poisoning:

The discomfort caused depends upon the amount toxins that are present in the body of the bird. There are some signs of toxicity that you need to watch out for:

- Shallow breathing
- Lethargy
- Anorexia
- Weight loss
- Weakness
- Kidney dysfunction
- Blue or purple coloration of the skin
- Feather picking
- Regurgitation
- Paleness in the mucous membrane
- Excessive consumption of water followed by urination to flush the toxins out.
- Inability to balance the body.

The most common sources of infection are the cages, toys and wires around the cage that are galvanized, washers or nuts made from zinc, pennies that were minted after the year 1983.

Lead poisoning:

Lead poisoning is more fatal as the lead that is absorbed will be retained in the soft tissues of the body. This can cause neural damage and can even lead to problems with the kidneys and the GI system.

The symptoms of lead poisoning are the same as zinc poisoning. But the sources of zinc poisoning are a lot more in comparison. The common sources are tooth brushes, lead paint, lead weight used for curtains, crystal, cardboard boxes, dyes used in newspaper, vinyl or plastic material, stainless glass windows, plumbing material, foils of some champagne bottles etc.

To treat this condition, an injection called Calsenate is administered. This acts like an antidote that will remove the zinc or lead that has entered the body. If the bird has ingested any metal object, it can be removed surgically. The bird must be put on a recommended diet to ensure that the kidneys and the liver do not shut down, making it harder for the metals to be eliminated from the body.

Make sure that your bird is in a safe environment in order to prevent any metal poisoning. If you are unsure of how to do this on your own, you have several professionals who can come to your home and take care of the whole bird proofing process for you.

**Feather plucking**

This is often considered a behavioral disorder but can also be associated with several physiological conditions that cause extreme discomfort to the bird.

Feather plucking is a form of self-mutilation where the bird plucks the skin off his body, leading to large bald patches and also infections due to the wounds caused by plucking. The causes for feather plucking are many, including:

- **Malnutrition:** When major nutrients like magnesium and calcium are absent from the bird's diet, it can lead to irritation of the skin, forcing the bird to pluck at the feathers.
- **Allergies:** If your bird is allergic to any foods or preservatives, he may resort to feather plucking.
- **Boredom:** When Scarlet Macaws do not get the necessary amount of exercise and mental stimulation they get extremely bored and will choose feather plucking as a form of entertainment.
- **Light:** Scarlet Macaws require a good amount of sunlight. If you keep the cage in a dark corner of your home, the bird will develop Vitamin D deficiency which makes him vulnerable to feather plucking. You can see a complete change in the way your bird behaves with a simple change in the availability of natural light.

One medicine that is effective in controlling the condition is Clomipramine, which helps in the regrowth of feathers. The inflammation in the affected areas is also reduced, making the bird reduce the action of plucking feathers.

In case of stress induced feather plucking, it is possible to treat the condition effectively with antidepressants, hypnotics and sedatives. This is required if you travel with the bird, introduce another bird or make changes in the routine of the bird. Any form of change in the immediate environment or shock can make your bird vulnerable to feather plucking.

It is important for you to spend as much time with your bird as possible. Feather clipping is a great measure to prevent escapes or flight related injuries. However, it is a rather big setback for the bird. Flying is the best form of exercise for the bird and also keeps him entertained. Of course a housing area that is too small for the bird to fly is also a bad idea.

You need to make sure that your Scarlet Macaw is stimulated mentally as well. This includes buying him a lot of toys or even providing him with homemade foraging toys that keep him engaged.

Spending time with your bird can act as the best measure against feather plucking in most cases. Train the bird, play with him or simply talk to him for a few minutes. These birds are extremely social and a lack of bonding with a mate or the flock will make them behave differently.

If everything fails, you need to make sure that your bird is checked by a vet for any other internal conditions or infections. In this case, feather plucking is merely a symptom and not a behavioral condition. It can be controlled by treated the causal health problem.

## 3. Accidents and Injuries

Accidents are very common with birds, especially when they are able to fly. There could be additional problems like fights within the flock, sudden aggression due to breeding seasons, feather clipping accidents or poisoning that require immediate attention.

These emergencies require you to provide the right type of first aid in order to prevent any untoward effects on the bird. There are a few common problems that you may have to face when you have a bird at home:

**Broken blood feathers**

When the blood feather is broken, a lot of blood is lost. This is not a cause for concern as long as the bird is given the right treatment to prevent bleeding. The best thing to do would be to apply light pressure on the affected area and apply some flour on the area. You can keep it covered with gauze until you reach the veterinarian. In most case, the blood feather will be pulled out.

## Wounds and abrasions

Birds may have some wounds on the surface of the skin. Normally, wounds and abrasions are superficial and can be managed with some simple cleaning with hydrogen peroxide or betadine. If there is any dirt on the wound, you can get rid of it with a pair of tweezers. Then, you may apply some antibiotic ointment as a preventive measure. Make sure that the bird does not pick at the wound. If it is deep and has exposed the flesh, you need to see a veterinarian immediately.

## Attacks by dogs or cats

Scarlet Macaws are large birds. However, they are also easily stressed when an animal like a dog goes after them. If this happens, you need to remain extremely calm and keep the bird in a quiet place to prevent further stress.

The next thing to do would be to check for the damage on the body. In case of any broken wings or bones, all you need to do is tie it to the body of the bird with gauze lightly. This will prevent any movement and further damage. In case of any damage to the skull or the legs, you will have to call your veterinarian home.

Cat and dog saliva can be toxic for birds. Therefore, it is a must that you have the bird checked even if the injuries are minute. This prevents any chances of bacterial infections or other infections.

## Tongue bleeding

The tongue of a bird has several blood vessels and can be damaged sometimes due to toys or even while climbing. You will notice that the tongue bleeds quite profusely. So you will have to make sure that you see a vet immediately. You cannot use a styptic pencil in this case. Even flour can choke the bird.

## Bleeding toenails

This is quite common as birds can have their toenails stuck in upholstery or on your shirt and just have them rip off when they are trying to fly away. This is not a very serious condition as it can be managed with a simple dab of the styptic pencil. It is when the bleeding is unstoppable that you should take the bird to the vet immediately.

## Labored breathing

If your bird is experiencing any shortness of breath or is wheezing while inhaling, it is a sign of some form of nasal blockage.

The first thing you need to do is check if there are any blockages in the nasal passage. In case of any dried mucus, you can just wipe it off with a wet cloth. Other obstructions include seeds or parts of toys. Do not try to remove it yourself if you notice it as you may harm the bird. Take him to a vet immediately.

Open mouth breathing or panting can be caused by overheating of the body. This could be because of travelling, exercise or even a change in the temperature. If this is ignored, the bird may have a heat stroke. You will notice that the bird will stretch its wings out, breathe very heavily and just collapse in case of a heatstroke.

In this case, the bird must immediately be shifted to a cooler place. Hold a cold towel around the body of the bird. In case the bird is able to stand, you can even get him to stand in a shallow bowl of cold water.

Shortness of breath could be an indication of several other diseases. Therefore, make sure you consult your vet immediately.

## Burns

If the bird lands on a hot stove or a hot pan, he can have severe burns. Sometimes even the radiator can lead to burns. You need to make sure that the affected area is washed immediately with cold water. Then, using clean gauze, wipe the area dry gently. Cold compress is the best remedy for mild burns.

In case of any severe burns, you will have to take your bird to the emergency room or consult your vet immediately. These birds tend to go into extreme shock and will need care immediately. Most often, besides the topical treatment, antibiotics are administered to prevent any infections of the wounds.

## Chilling

Birds like the Scarlet Macaw are from the tropics and will not be able to handle very cold temperatures. It is mandatory to keep them in a warm area. Sometimes, you may even have to use a heat lamp to keep the temperatures up.

If your bird is suffering from chilling, you will have to supply heat to the body with a warm towel or even a heat lamp that is set to about 90 degrees Fahrenheit. Chilling can be caused by shock or injury and it requires immediate medical attention in that case. Environmental changes, drafts and even very cold air conditioning can lead to chilling.

### a. Preparing a first aid kit

A first aid kit is a must in a home with any pets. In case of birds, too, you need to prepare a first aid kit that can help you provide emergency care to the bird when required. The items you need to include are:

- The number and directions to your veterinary clinic or the emergency facility suggested by your avian vet.
- Phone numbers for poison control. You will be able to get this information from your vet.
- Scissors in order to remove any strings or to cut bandaging material.
- Sterilized gauze
- Q-tips to clean up a wound and to apply any topical medicine.
- Tape
- A roll of clean gauze to wrap a wing that is injured.
- Antibiotic cream recommended by the vet.
- Styptic pencil to control bleeding.
- Betadine or Hydrogen peroxide to clean any wound.
- Pliers or tweezers to handle small bandages and tapes.
- Heating pad to help a bird experiencing chilling.
- An ink dropper to administer internal medication.
- Large towels to handle the bird.
- Thermometer to measure the temperature of the bird's body.

Keep all of the above in a box that is easily accessible and make sure that your family is aware of the different situations that may require the first aid kit. They also need to be told how the bird can be helped in case of common accidents and injuries around the house.

# 4. Preventive Measures

Prevention is always better than cure. It is really heartbreaking to see your beloved pet wallow in pain and die an unexpected death. Instead of multiple veterinary meetings, it is a good idea to take a few simple preventive measures to keep your birds safe:

• **Keep them away from wild birds or animals:** The cage should be kept in an area that is not accessible to any wild birds or rodents like mice that generally carry a lot of disease causing microbes. The food and water, especially should not be contaminated by them. Any spilled food or litter should be cleaned up immediately to make sure that these creatures are not attracted.

• **Clean up as much as you can:** The housing area of the bird must be pristine. The most common breeding grounds for bacteria, parasites and viruses include organic matter in the cage such as the feces.

Make sure that the cage is cleaned on a regular basis. You need to be additionally cautious if you are planning to keep the birds outdoors.

You must make it a rule not to borrow equipment or allow other bird owners to handle your macaw. This can lead to the transmission of unwanted feather dander or microbe carrying debris.

• **Keep an eye on your bird:** Be an attentive bird parent. If your Scarlet Macaw shows the slightest deviation from what you consider normal, become alert. You may have to take your bird to the vet to have him examined completely. It may seem like you are too overprotective at times. However, it is necessary that you catch any disease as early as you can to provide suitable treatment to help the bird cope with it and recover fast.

• **Follow good quarantining:** Make sure that any new bird that is included in the flock is quarantined properly. Most often, a bird could simply be a carrier of the condition. When kept in quarantine, you will be able to observe the bird for any abnormality. This can be treated effectively before it spreads to other birds in your household. Even if you plan to take your bird to shows or exhibitions, you will have to quarantine him for at least two weeks before reintroducing him to the flock. A great way to ensure that your bird is not a carrier is to find a good breeder who practices strict disease control at his center.

• **Regular vet visits:** Your bird needs to be checked regularly for any chance of infections. Make sure that you never miss your annual veterinary checkup if you want to keep your bird in good health at all times. Here are a few recommended tests that you should have the vet conduct to be sure that your bird is free from deadly diseases:

**Adult birds:**
- Complete blood count to make sure that there are no internal infections.
- Study of culture to diagnose any possibility of yeast or bacterial infection.
- Full body X-ray.

**Young birds:**
- Complete Blood Count to check for any internal infection.
- Chlamydophilia Immunoassay in order to diagnose parrot fever that is highly contagious.
- Culture study to eliminate chances of yeast or bacterial infections.

You can never be too sure of the right methods to take good care of your bird. However, you can be a good parent by eliminating all the chances of the disease and reduce the risk for your beloved Scarlet Macaw. With these preventive measures you can take care of most deadly conditions easily.

# Conclusion

Thank you for putting your faith in this book. Hopefully, all your queries about handling a Scarlet Macaw have been answered effectively. As you bond with your bird and learn more about him, your knowledge will automatically surge. Until then, this book is meant to serve as the first step towards learning about bird care.

Since the book is based on experiences of other Scarlet Macaw owners, you can be certain that all the information is authentic and practical. That way, you will be able to identify the problem easily and apply the suggested solution.

If this book has helped you make decision about purchasing the bird, then my work is done. Whether you decided to go for a Scarlet Macaw or not, you have made a good choice. If you are honestly unable to take care of the bird, then it is best to avoid stress to the bird as well as yourself.

However, if you did choose to bring a bird home, you must know that your life has changed forever. You will find the best companion in your Scarlet Macaw. These birds are extremely loving and affectionate and are worth all the efforts you put in.

# References

You need to keep yourself updated with all the information available about Scarlet Macaws. Of course, the Internet is the best place to look as it is loaded with interesting forums, blogs and websites that can provide you with all the info you need about Scarlet Macaws. You will even get to interact with parrot owners who have dedicated their lives to providing a loving home for their feathered friends.

Note: at the time of printing, all the websites below were working. As the Internet changes rapidly, some sites might no longer be live when you read this book. That is, of course, out of my control.

Here are a few links that you can refer to:

www.trainedparrot.com/Socialization

www.rainforest-alliance.org/kids/species-profiles/macaw

www.thearaproject.org/about/background/

www.osaconservation.org

www.horniman.ac.uk

www.interesting-animal-facts.com

www.parrotsdailynews.com

www.bluemacaws.org

www.what-when-how.com

www.upatsix.com

www.animals.nationalgeographic.com

www.birdchannel.com

www.Scarlets.com

www.beautyofbirds.com

www.premiumparrots.com

www.lafeber.com

www.bagheera.com

www.thegabrielfoundation.org

www.peteducation.com

www.animal-world.com

www.petparrot.com

www.parrotsecrets.com

www.birdtricks.com

www.au.answers.yahoo.com

www.neotropical.birds.cornell.edu

www.rioyou.blogspot.in

www.avianadventuresaviary.com

www.itis.gov

www.Scarletmacawaviary.com

www.funtimebirdy.wordpress.com

www.studentswithbirds.wordpress.com

www.parrotislandinc.com

www.parrotsinternational.org